Night and Day Prayer
ACCORDING TO DAVID

Night and Day Prayer
ACCORDING TO DAVID

By Laird Pearcy

XULON PRESS

Xulon Press
2301 Lucien Way #415
Maitland, FL 32751
407.339.4217
www.xulonpress.com

Printed in the United States of America.

Paperback ISBN-13: 978-1-6312-9492-1

eBook ISBN-13: 978-1-6312-9493-8

DEDICATION

On August 15, 2003, I had a dream that sent ripples across my life. In the dream, I was informed that I was required to complete a forty-day layoff by December 31, 2003—at the time, I worked for a large, national company. In the dream, I asked several folks for confirmation of this layoff. Some in the company had already started to take their forty days—splitting a week, three days on, two off, and so forth. Apparently, I was a little late in getting the message. I awoke from this intense dream and shared it with my wife, Anne. With little hesitation, she replied that I was being invited to fast for forty days for spiritual breakthrough in whatever manner I could before the specified deadline. I was speechless. That was not the confirmation I was looking for—I'm dreadful at fasting! But in the end, I accepted God's invitation.

During that season of fasting, I attended a conference in Kansas City, Missouri, sponsored by the International House of Prayer (IHOPKC). Anne had already attended several IHOPKC women's conferences and always came back with wonderful reports. She loved what she heard from Mike Bickle, the director of IHOPKC. He was passionate for Jesus and committed to strong Biblical teaching. It was my first exposure to the House of Prayer movement, and nothing in my pastoral training had prepared me for this new paradigm.

I began to read and study all that I could find on it. I was aware of other prayer movements in history and was surprised that I hadn't heard more about this before. I found myself asking the question, "Is this really in the Bible?"

IHOPKC's key verse is Psalm 27:4, spoken by King David: "One thing I have asked from the LORD, that I shall seek: That I may dwell in the house of the LORD all the days of my life, To behold the beauty of the LORD And to meditate in His temple."

Mike Bickle believed he had received a mandate from the Lord to establish a House of Prayer where this verse could be fulfilled, a place that would be open 24/7 with singers and musicians, as described in 1 Chronicles 23 and 25. The Kansas City Prayer Room opened in September 1999. It has been running 24/7 for twenty-plus years and has seen over 20 million hours of prayers prayed, declared, and sung. It is really quite remarkable.

I believe you will find, as I did, the answer to my question was a resounding, "Yes, it is indeed in the Bible."

I would like to dedicate this book to Mike Bickle and the thousands of intercessory missionaries and worshippers who have passed through the doors of the International House of Prayer in Kansas City. They have given themselves to prayer, fasting, and worship 24/7 in anticipation of the greatest move of God on the earth and the long-awaited return of His beloved Son!

TABLE OF CONTENTS

Foreword

It has been God's intention from the beginning of creation for man to dwell with Him. It has been man's struggle since the fall to accept God's invitation and to know how to dwell with Him.

This book is a careful biblical study of the roots of today's House of Prayer movement. Laird has developed a strong argument for the restoration of *David's fallen tent* (Acts 15:16) in our day. His deep dive into key Hebrew words and phrases is compelling. My understanding of the call and the work of prayer has forever changed.

This book is a wonderful challenge for today's believer to get serious about the joyous and satisfying pursuit of prayer with God in the company of singers and musicians. It is an invitation across all denominations to seek the intimacy and partnership with God that we have been made for.

"My eyes shall be upon the faithful of the land that they may dwell with me; He who walks in a blameless way is the one who will minister to me" (Ps. 101:6).

> *—Anne Pearcy, wife, mother, grandmother*
> *and one who joyously dwells with God*

ACKNOWLEDGMENTS

Writing always seemed to me to be something others did. I have found myself surprised over the past fifteen years to be driven to write. And although professional editors would eventually do final work on my manuscript, it was my wife, Anne, daughters, Jody Striker and Karyn McDonald and a few faithful friends who did the initial reads of my raw material. Special thanks to Gwen Gornicki and Pam Lantz for your valuable suggestions and editing. That was enormously helpful to me!

PREFACE

I n most competitions, strategy changes as the game clock runs down. Sometimes this shift in strategy is dramatic and surprising. It may be a special play, a sudden burst of energy, or even just staying steady that ensures the winning outcome. Olympians, professional athletes and even the youngest upcoming stars know this well.

God's restoration of David's practice of *intercessory worship* is an end-time strategy and game changer. Davidic worship (also known as intercessory worship) refers to the night and day corporate offering that mixes instrumentally supported worship and intercession before the face of the Lord, according to the heavenly pattern given King David (1 Chron. 28:19). It is agreement with God in declaration and song. Worship (declaring God's attributes) and intercession (declaring God's purposes in the earth) flow from the Scriptures (God's testimony). The worshipers remind God what He has written and promised in His Word and they call forth its fulfillment. This offering of worship and intercession from the forgiven and intimate hearts of the worshipers engenders in the Master Himself an astounding and deeply satisfying joy. This service *to* and joyful experience *of* the Master is called the *sharath* (Hebrew) of the Lord, which in turn drives a missions outreach to the nations—drawing all men with marvelous signs—to come in awe and dwell in His courts. This book will explore the development of Davidic worship.

David was given a revelation of God's House and its operation, and it was so much more than what Moses had been given. As a result, David appointed 288 prophetic singers, 4,000 band members, and 4,000 gatekeepers to provide perpetual worship and intercession before the Lord who was seated above the mercy seat on the Ark of the Covenant between the cherubim's outstretched wings. David set up a simple tent for this purpose. In the Psalms, David asked that his prayer would be as incense before the Lord and the lifting up of his hands (worship) as an offering (Ps.141:2). Transition from Moses to David was in the air, but it would not be until David's heir, Jesus, died and rose again that the transition would be completed. Is it possible God has something amazing He wants to bring back from the past to usher in the end times?

God is moving the church toward the finish line and a great final harvest. He is calling forth the church, His bride, to be fully in love with Jesus and ready for His return. This is the call of houses of prayer all over the world—calling believers into intimacy with their Bridegroom God and partnership though prayer in all that He is doing.

Chapter One

BACK TO FRONT

R evelation is the last book of the Bible, written by the apostle John and is traditionally set around AD 95. It is the last written revelation of Jesus directed by Jesus Himself (Rev. 1:1), and in that sense is the last words and testimony of Jesus. The bulk of John's book appears to disclose God's battle plans for the end of the age and the long-awaited age to come. What John saw was difficult to put into words. No doubt some elements were familiar to him, and he had language to describe them. Other elements were simply fantastic. He did the best he could with what he had to describe what he saw.

The goal in this apologetic is not to understand and comprehensively interpret what John saw. There are many fine commentaries available and numerous perspectives and interpretations offered for that purpose. The focus of this book, rather, is to take a step back and look at what he saw as it relates to *Night and Day Prayer According to David*.

Sometimes the best way to understand a dramatic story is to start at the last chapter and work your way back to the beginning. Those who love a good story would be appalled at this approach. In the case of understanding the biblical framework for night and day prayer, starting with the end of the story helps us frame the conversation and fit the puzzle pieces together once they have been gathered from our study.

Near the end of the book of Revelation, John records seeing the bride (Rev. 19:7-8). She is ready for the marriage supper of the Lamb. The earliest reference to the bride and Bridegroom actually appears in John's gospel account of the beginning of Jesus's ministry. In that account, many were coming to Jesus to be baptized and one of John the Baptist's disciples was concerned. John saw his disciple's troubled look and remarked that he himself was not the Christ. Jesus was the rightful Bridegroom and the bride would belong to Him. John was only the friend of the Bridegroom (John 3:26-29).

In his time, the apostle John knew what a bride was. Every reader of John's account, regardless of culture, has some familiarity with what it means to be a bride. She is a universal symbol. John also knew about the groom, the one whom John the Baptist called "Lamb of God" (John 1:29). Before his heavenly revelation, the apostle John had written about Him in his gospel. He knew the groom, and he knew the bride. John had seen first-hand the bride's struggle from the early days of Jesus's ministry to the time of His urgent report sent to the seven Asian churches. The gospels and epistles record her successes and disappointments.

The apostle John didn't use this term again until he wrote about his revelation, beginning with the events surrounding the city of Babylon—the archenemy of Jerusalem. It will be destroyed as a city and will no longer have commerce or revelry. The natural voice of the bride and Bridegroom will no longer be heard in Babylon (Rev. 18:23). Marriage celebration in that city will cease.

Jesus will appear in the sky with His vast army when the final battle of Armageddon is fought. The Antichrist's army will be destroyed, and the beast and the false prophet will be thrown into the lake of fire. Thrones of judgment will be set up. John saw the first resurrection, the 1,000-year reign, and the second death. Then he saw Jerusalem coming down as a bride adorned for her husband (Rev. 21:2). The angelic speaker took John to a high mountain to see the wife of the Lamb—the bride—Jerusalem coming down from heaven (Rev. 21:9-10). Why is Jerusalem so unique and warrant such mention? The Psalmist quoted David, who answered that question: God "has desired it for His habitation" (Ps. 132:13). God unconditionally gave land to Abraham (Gen. 15:17-18) and chose Jerusalem as His capital. He alone will refashion, adorn, and bring her to earth.

After Babylon has been crushed, a thunderous chorus from a great multitude in heaven will be heard applauding the bride, who is ready for the marriage feast (Rev. 19:7-8). The last reference occurs in the final chapter of the book of Revelation. Jesus (the descendent of David by the Spirit) and the bride issue an invitation to come (Rev. 22:17). Anyone who hears it will be welcome and should come. We turn our attention in this book to the bride of Christ—the saints.

The revelatory heavenly chorus provided John the signature statement on the bride. "'Let us rejoice and be glad and give the glory to Him, for the marriage of the Lamb has come and His bride has made herself ready.' It was given to her to clothe herself in fine linen, bright *and* clean; for the fine linen is the righteous acts of the saints" (Rev. 19:7-8). Good news! The bride made herself ready.

Presumably, she had not been ready up to this revealed future point, but now she was ready for the marriage of the Lamb. She had clothed herself in righteous acts, and the supper could start. The reader must first ask, "Why is Jesus using the bridal terminology as He views the saints?" and second, "How does this relate to night and day prayer?" The first question is addressed below, and the second will become clear later.

The language of the bride is an interpretive key. It is called the *bridal paradigm*. An example of an interpretive key related to today's standards would be as follows. The video player or gamer, as he is sometimes called, enters the computer game and must watch for and retrieve a key or some icon to play the game successfully. The game can progress without the key, but a negative outcome will eventually result. The player will either be eliminated or stuck on his current level. No matter how many times he restarts the game, he will lose. He must have the key to move forward, and he must pick up other keys as presented. It is built into the strategy of the game. Everything depends on it. The key allows the player access to hidden chambers or secret levels filled with provision—armaments, wealth, alliances, power, and strategies for the game's trip or objective. This is the almost universal approach to the computer games that have captured a generation of youth. You need the key to play and advance. Paying careful attention and watching for it is required.

Likewise, the bridal paradigm is just such a key to understanding all that God has done and will do. He is the

Bridegroom God, and we the saints are the bride. The significance of Jerusalem as bride—a city greatly desired by God—will be touched upon later. To better grasp the bridal paradigm, we will focus on the saints who are getting ready. God looks at us through this bridal lens, and we in turn need to look at Him this same way. Without this key, our difficulties in understanding the rest of scriptures will only increase, and like the computer gamer, the outcome is not one we will want. (see Rev 3:7)

God is spirit. John realized he was not receiving new information on the nature of God, but a powerful visual cue. All the bridal and marriage images likely flowed through his mind as he pondered what he saw. It is about relationship, intimacy, friendship, lifelong commitment, devotion, passion, time together, companionship, fascination, pursuit, and shared ministry. God wants a First Commandment heart because He is a First Commandment God. In the vision, John saw that the bride had become a First Commandment saint. She was ready when the marriage feast began. The bridal paradigm is not a means to an end. It is the destination.

The bridal paradigm reveals God's motivation, drive, and heart for us. It is the lens through which we should view ourselves before such a God. We are the apple of His eye (Zech. 2:8). We are saved by faith through the blood of the Lamb, sanctified and glorified. Throughout all eternity we will still be the bride, and God will always be the Bridegroom as His affection rests on us. The cry of the Reformation continues to be clear: Salvation is by faith alone. It was and is a bedrock statement. Yet John understood that eternity is set in the context of the bridal paradigm! This is not simply looking forward in time but backwards as well. It is eternal. God has never been less than the Bridegroom God with a desire for a bride. The revelation of this attribute was revealed slowly over the course of time, and John was given the last authoritative expression on this side of heaven.

The bride exerts effort in her relationship with the Groom. She prepares herself because she desires the Lord. The longing of a fascinated lover and partner is the heart's focus—not the work of a laborer who expects a wage. It is not a performance for show with accolades that follow. Lovers will always outdo and outlast those who expend themselves for any other reason. Lovers die for one another (John 10:12-13; John 15:13), whereas a laborer's effort is related to the value of the wage, and effort changes based on the perceived value of that wage. The laborer has limits. Self-preservation guides the effort. The lover operates differently.

John saw the marriage supper of the Lamb. This is the pinnacle of the bride's devotion and patient waiting. It is a celebration that will last forever.

God would have a bride and be a Bridegroom. If you become a Christian [or *saint*] under any other motivation, it must yield to the bridal paradigm. Avoiding hell, being delivered from addictions and sin, the desire to do good, making a righteous and true choice, and other rationales for coming to Christ are all valid reasons, but they must ultimately give way to the bridal paradigm. This eclipses all other motivations for coming into the kingdom, or doing the work of the kingdom.

How exactly does the bride who was revealed to John get ready? It is not a mystery, although the book of Revelation is a challenging read. John was an amazing recorder, but he also knew his Old Testament very well. His book is full of allusions to the Old Testament. Grant Osborne writes, "Everyone agrees that the OT is alluded to more often in the Apocalypse than in any other NT book but no one agrees about the exact number of allusions, because it is difficult to determine partial quotations, allusions, and echoes of the OT in the book" (Osborne, Revelation 2002, 25). It is impossible to understand the book of Revelation apart from the Old Testament, and the bride's actions to ready herself are more fully understood within the Old Testament context.

John has identified three saintly attributes or righteous acts of the saints. The first has already been given. She is a bride. She has become passionate and devoted. The other two will follow in the next chapter. However, before moving on to consider John's discovery, a word from the apostle Paul should be heard. It is an important elaboration on the bridal paradigm. Paul tells the Corinthians—and us today—that we must not be unequally yoked in marriage (2 Cor. 6:14-17 KJV). We are not to marry an unbeliever.

This seems like a simple directive, but over time, the definition of a "believer" has become so broad it is almost meaningless. Scripture is clear on the matter of being unequally yoked, and God applies the scripture to Himself. He will not give His matchless, sinless Son to a bride who is not equally passionate and dedicated to God's things. If the bride is uncertain about her bridal qualifications, she should look at the Son for a point of reference. She must be like Him, and Jesus promises this to John (1 John 3:2). The Son of God will not be unequally yoked! This is a warning as well as a promise. Understanding God's commitment to His matchless Son makes the bride's readiness all the more amazing.

Chapter Two

GETTING READY

Our search to help unravel these bridal attributes or righteous acts and clues about the bridal paradigm will take us to Moses (Chapter Four of this book) and eventually to David (Chapter Eight), who figures prominently in this paradigm. If you flip back several chapters from Revelation 19:7, you will discover one of the actions the bride has taken. She has gained a testimony. She has become a witness. She is the bride with a testimony.

> Then I heard a loud voice in heaven, saying, Now the salvation, and the power, and the kingdom of our God and the authority of His Christ have come, for the accuser of our brethren has been thrown down, he who accuses them before our God day and night. And they overcame him because of the blood of the Lamb and because of the word of their testimony, and they did not love their life even when faced with death. (Rev. 12:10-11)

John is told that the bride (brethren) was able to overcome the accuser of the brethren (Satan) because of what the Lamb has done with His blood and because of her testimony. She has something to say. The bride's testimony is so fixed in her spirit and life that she will not yield even when faced with death. This book will touch on how the bride gains such a testimony.

Curiously, the word used for testimony is a form of the Greek word *marturia*, from which the English term martyr is derived. A testimony has that understanding built in and is what you will die for. It is also translated *witness* or *reputation*. The bride has a corresponding reputation for the message she carries. She is a witness, and she witnesses before God, man, and the angelic beings—even Satan.

John discovers that Satan accuses the brethren day and night. God's heavenly courts are open around the clock to receive accusations and are open as well to receive the testimonies or godly declarations of the saints. Satan has had freedom to enter the courts day and night to make his case. He is not summarily thrown out for daring to come before the King. The church, however, has been reluctant to testify in God's courts during the late watches of the night. She has ceded to the enemy this territory on which he has effectively trespassed. King David's counsel will be helpful. It may well be that Satan is thrown out because the bride finally takes her rightful place in the Bridegroom's courthouse day and night. Satan will no longer be uncontested and free to vomit up his accusations.

As John listens to the speaker announce the arrival of the marriage supper of the Lamb, he is overwhelmed. "Then I fell at his feet to worship him. But he said to me, 'Do not do that; I am a fellow servant of yours and your brethren who hold the testimony of Jesus; worship God. For the testimony of Jesus is the spirit of prophecy'" (Rev. 19:10). The bride doesn't have a separate testimony after all. It is not unique to her. Rather, she shares in the testimony of Jesus along with the rest of the heavenly host. The testimony of Jesus is the root of what the prophets and now the apostles have been proclaiming all along. It has a context and content. It is grounded in the scriptures. The bride finally adopts His testimony and makes it her own. She speaks and declares what God Himself declares.

What is this testimony? It is Jesus. Jesus is the crux of Christianity. All the cults and false religions stumble over Jesus. He was and is fully God (Col. 2:9) and fully man (Phil. 2:5-8). To the natural man, this is incomprehensible: He must be one or the other; or He only seems like one; or He is a composite of the two, like an epoxy glue that mixes glue and hardener together in the right proportion to get a bond. Christianity has always maintained that Jesus was 100 percent of both, not a mixture. He doesn't just *appear* to have characteristics of both: He was and is seamlessly both. Because He is fully God and fully man, Jesus was and is fully spiritual and fully natural.

He operates comfortably in both realms and expects His bride to do likewise. This often causes consternation at some level for His disciples, who responded like the cults at first. They wanted to know, "How am I to live?" "Is my life to be lived in spiritual ecstasy while my body languishes, or do I become engaged in the business of life and fit in my spiritual aspirations when I can?" The Lord's answer is more complex. We, like Him, must be fully natural and fully spiritual.

We too must operate comfortably in both realms. The mathematics of this is impossible. One plus one equals two, not one. Yet, this is the substance of His testimony. Jesus was born in a manger, able to share a meal with friends, create a good deal of wine for a marriage celebration, heal the sick, and raise the dead. He is fully natural and fully spiritual. This is the core of the gospel.

This impossible dynamic is only made possible by the Spirit of God living in us (1 Cor. 3:16). Christ died for sin that this might be so (2 Cor. 5:15-21). The body of Christ does not like the implications, preferring to live closer to the middle than at the ends where fanatics often dwell—not too spiritual and not too worldly. We think like the manufacturer of that epoxy glue. You need a 50/50 blend to get the right bond. While this is true for epoxy glue, it is not so for Christians. Such a blend is known as the Laodicean approach to Christianity, and in the end is a bad strategy (Rev. 3:14-22). Our testimony is fully natural and fully spiritual, just like Jesus.

The testimony of Jesus first became noticeable with Moses when the term *testimony* was introduced. A more comprehensive description of His developing testimony will be addressed in Chapter Four.

She is the bride with a testimony, and she prays a lot. This next important righteous action taken by the bride—that being prayer—is found in Revelation 5:8. The elders are standing before the Lord in His throne room just prior to the release of the seal, trumpet, and bowl judgments. In one hand, they have musical instruments, and in the other they have golden bowls filled with incense, which, John is told, is the prayers of the saints. The bride has been praying a lot.

She is His friend and companion, has the testimony of Jesus, is fully natural and fully spiritual, and prays relentlessly and with purpose to fill those bowls.

Jesus takes the scroll from the Father's hand because it was time to release His judgments. "When He had taken the book, the four living creatures and the twenty-four elders fell down before the Lamb, each one holding a harp and golden bowls full of incense, which are the prayers of the saints" (Rev. 5:8). One may ask, "Why do the elders have musical instruments in one hand and bowls in the other?" John tells us that the incense in the bowls are the prayers of the saints. And we learn from verse 9 that the elders are singing a new song. This is a striking picture of instrumentally assisted worship and intercession before the Lord. This will be better understood once we have introduced David's vision in Chapter Nine.

No information is provided on whether personal or corporate prayer fills the bowls. It is probably both, although the corporate setting of the heavenly scene suggests that the more difficult of the two types of prayer—corporate prayer—is in focus. We are not told if this is prayer from the past, present, or future. It is probably all three. Given the placement in John's story, it may well be the prayers of the *last days*—the end of the age—are most in view. John did not record the exact nature of the bride's offered prayers. However, since they are the bride's prayers, they are most likely related to Matthew 6:10 (where Jesus instructed the disciples how to pray). The bride wants the kingdom to function on earth as it does in heaven. And she longs for the presence of her Groom and the release of His righteousness and justice throughout the land.

For John, prayer is not just the warm-up to the beginning of a series of judgments; rather, it sustains and even propels those judgments. As the scenes of judgment are presented to John, he sees even more prayer.

Regardless of one's view of the last days or how to interpret the book of Revelation, it is clear at the beginning of the seal judgments that the golden bowls are full. A tipping point has been reached and the very next prayer will cause an overflow. The final countdown to the marriage supper has begun.

War and its various attributes are released in the first four seals of Revelation chapter six. The Conqueror, the sword to slay, famine, and death are all commanded to come; one-quarter of the world dies. The first four judgment seals make sense together, but it is difficult for the reader to understand how the prayers of the martyrs—those who call upon the name of the Lord—operate like a judgment. However, the prayers of the martyrs are a seal that is released. "And they cried out with a loud voice, saying, 'How long, O Lord, holy and true, will You refrain from judging and avenging our blood on those who dwell on the earth?'" (Rev. 6:10). Those prayers touch His heart. The Bridegroom takes action. The sixth seal judgment follows—every mountain moves, the stars fall from the sky, and everyone remaining hides (Rev. 6:12-17). It has a devastating effect. Prayer does not stop with the martyrs. It continues to flow in.

The trumpet judgment series are next (Rev. 8:2) and are more severe than the seals. John watches as the Lord adds incense; more prayer apparently has come in and adds to what the saints originally provided to launch the seals and what the martyrs brought in. The turbocharged trumpet judgments roll down. Prayer, as it was for the seals (Rev. 5:8), not only appears to be a triggering element in the trumpet judgments, but an accelerant as well. The angel in Revelation 8:5 takes fire from the incense altar (the place where prayer ascends before the Lord), places it in his censer, and sends the whole thing to earth. The next round of calamitous judgment begins.

No doubt John was mesmerized by what he saw. At the beginning of the sixth trumpet, John sees and hears an angelic announcement: "Then the sixth angel sounded, and I heard a voice from the four horns of the golden altar which is before God, one saying to the sixth angel who had the trumpet, 'Release the four angels who are bound at the great river Euphrates'" (Rev. 9:13-15).

The golden altar before God is the incense altar (Ex. 30:1-3). The command coming from the angel next to the altar of incense or place of prayer (Ps. 141:2) suggests an ongoing relationship between the prayers of the saints and the progression of the trumpet judgments and angelic announcements. The identity of the voice is not provided, but it is not hard to imagine the collective voice of prayer driving the outcome. At a minimum, the close association of the commanding voice and the altar of incense is telling.

This angel presumably continues to collect even more prayer that has come in. The incense angel releases four other angels who were bound at the great river Euphrates, and they are sent out to kill. One-half the world's population is now gone—a staggering loss. God must remove those who refuse the Bridegroom. His justice and righteousness must be satisfied, but His passion, His heart, and His consuming love and desire for His bride impels Him to remove all hindrances to His planned marriage feast. Judgment and justice will begin to roll down. The winepress of God's wrath is ready (Rev. 14:18-19). The *tares* must be removed (Matt. 13:29-30) and the wheat brought into His storehouse (Matt. 3:12).

The stage for the final battle is set. At the last trumpet, the heavenly Ark appears in the temple among the chorus of loud voices and declarations of the elders:

> Saying, We give You thanks, O Lord God, the Almighty, who are and who were, because You have taken Your great power and have begun to reign. And the nations were enraged, and Your wrath came, and the time *came* for the dead to be judged, and *the time* to reward Your bond-servants the prophets and the saints and those who fear Your name, the small and the great, and to destroy those who destroy the earth. (Rev. 11:17-18)

God's character is esteemed and His purposes are upheld. Everyone in the heavenly audience agrees with God. It is a tremendous testimony.

The heavenly altar continues to be active as the revelatory scenes roll on. It is involved in the bowls judgment (Rev. 16:7) and in the gathering of the cluster of ripened grapes for the winepress of God's wrath. From John's perspective, prayer—whether offered in the natural or heavenly realm—is intimately connected to the timing and outcome of the recorded events. Prayer is no small matter. It is not the condiment on the table of the Lord, but the main meal!

John sees that the bride has gotten herself ready. She is in love, praying relentlessly in the context of worship, and has the testimony of Jesus, but John must have been startled by the extent of the makeover. She had significant roadblocks to overcome.

Chapter Three

THE BRIDE'S DILEMMA

John understood that there will be a bride. The revelation was not just a warning, but much more a promise: The outcome is certain. At the time of his revelation, John was condemned to live on a penal colony off the coast of Ephesus. It was late in his life. And now, according to Jesus, the churches in several Asian cities where he had ministered are not doing well. The saints are struggling. In Jesus's summary (Rev. 2-3), there are some positive behaviors, but many more negative ones. The saints are being offered an invitation by the Bridegroom God to overcome and be the bride—even the lukewarm believers from Laodicea receive the invitation. The promise available is tremendous and the warning equally so. An adverse response could sadly cause Jesus to remove the lampstand of a city (Rev. 2:5). Curiously, Jesus addresses His message to churches in seven specific cities rather than giving a general message to all saints. The gap between where the churches were and where they need to be may seem large, but the Bridegroom God will intervene. There will be a bride for His matchless Son!

To reach the marriage supper of the Lamb in Revelation 19, the bride must overcome several obstacles. She is represented in John's account by the seven citywide churches of Asia. The first and foremost obstacle is that the bride, who is by very definition a lover, has left behind her first love (Rev. 2:4). Intimacy and friendship—the very foundation of being a bride—has been lost. She is busy, but she is no longer pursuing the great devotion. Note that the very first church to be reviewed and the very first problem identified is lost first love. This initial placement in the passage has significance. It is the primary problem—no intimacy. By extension, something else has replaced that first love. In essence, she is an adulterer. She is unsuitable for the Bridegroom in that condition.

But there is more. The bride, collectively speaking, has huge character defects. She has embraced immorality in both the natural and spiritual realms (Rev. 2:14, 20). She has a reputation for being spiritual, but she is actually dead (Rev. 3:1). She is disengaged from spiritual reality and believes she needs nothing (Rev. 3:17). Her testimony is marred. She is many brides instead of one bride for one groom. She is far from ready. Apparently the Laodicean church is not listening or speaking to Him, because Jesus counsels them to engage with Him. Sadly, prayer is not even mentioned in the Asian churches of John's day. He argues for the centrality of prayer for all the saints in the following chapters of his revelation. Today's challenge of prayerlessness will be examined in Chapter Twenty-Two.

John's revelation has truth for all generations, but is uniquely positioned for the last days generation and the events that dominate his book. Today, the church in the West, like the Laodicean church, contributes little to the golden bowls of incense, nor is she motivated to do so. Without the passion of the bride for the Bridegroom and with a marred reputation and little or no testimony, she can only stay busy with other things. She is not able to pray fervently or withstand the last days' events, much less help steer these events through prayer. In her present condition, she is unequally yoked to the Son and consequently unsuitable. She is trapped and requires deliverance. God's intervention is needed.

Is it possible that what will hasten the day of the Lord has been revealed in the book of Revelation? The apostle Peter told his followers the day could be hastened. The saints control the activity of filling the bowls with prayer, and developing the intimacy and testimony necessary for the bride's readiness.

God has left footprints in the sand the church must follow to rediscover intimacy, character, night and day testimony, and the prayer that will fill the golden bowls. He has begun to nudge His servants around the world to see them, and this nudge is quickly becoming more forceful. Having an equally yoked bride is paramount. God will not change His mind. He will change the church. The bride will have a change of heart, and with God's help will get herself ready. Participating thoughtfully with God is always better than being taken by surprise. It is God's heart to do nothing without first announcing His plans to His prophets (Amos 3:7).

For John, the solution appears to be found in Revelation 4-5. We will look at these two chapters later in this book (Chapter Twenty-One). In the book of Revelation, John provides many allusions to the Old Testament to help us track down and capture God's solution to lost intimacy, bad testimony, and prayerlessness. God laid these down long ago.

Without the Old Testament, it is impossible to understand the book of Revelation and the bride's restoration. Recovery begins in the garden.

Chapter Four

THE GARDEN; ABRAHAM, MOSES, AND THE ARK— FRIENDSHIP WITH GOD

T he creation story is familiar to most. Adam and Eve, our first parents, turned away from the Lord and began a life of great difficulty for themselves and their offspring. Satan was instrumental in playing the right note to catch their hearts and turn them. As the first sin was coming to light, Moses gives us this snapshot. "They heard the sound of the LORD God walking in the garden in the cool of the day, and the man and his wife hid themselves from the presence of the LORD God among the trees of the garden" (Gen. 3:8). The image of God walking in the garden in the cool of the day is reminiscent perhaps of other days in that garden when fellowship was intact. Adam and Eve hiding is the first clue in scripture that a great loss of intimacy has occurred. God promises restoration. The enemy will lose, but Adam and Eve have suffered the loss of intimacy. The story of restoration now begins.

God began to unfold His plan. Adam's descendants increased but for the most part grew increasingly evil. By the time of Noah, dramatic action was needed. Only Noah and his family were saved in the deluge God released (Gen. 7:1). Noah and his sons started again, and Adam's line survived and grew. The story continued with Abram, who was called out of Ur and migrated to Canaan, coming to Shechem where God appeared to him and promised to give the land to Abram's descendants. Abram journeyed further to Bethel, where he built an altar to the Lord and called on the name of the Lord (Gen. 12:8). Bethel means *house of God*. Abram became Abraham, for he was to be a father to a multitude of nations (Gen. 17:5). His direct line of descendants would come through Isaac and become a mighty nation, and all the other nations would be blessed through him as well (Gen. 18:18). They would experience a measure of Abraham's fathering.

Abraham's grandson, Jacob came to Bethel years later and had a powerful experience (Gen. 28:12) when God appeared to him and restated His promise given to Abraham. "Then Jacob awoke from his sleep and said, 'Surely the LORD is in this place, and I did not know it.' He was afraid and said, 'How awesome is this place! This is none other than the house of God, and this is the gate of heaven'" (Gen. 28:16-17). Bethel's significance declined over time. Jeroboam, king of Israel, went there years later and set up his idolatrous calf, making it a high place and a royal residence (Amos 7:13). But God provided a key insight to His house. It is place of awe, a gate of heaven, and a place to call on God. Moses, the prophets, and David would have more to say about God's House while calling on Him.

This restoration story picks up with Moses and the Ark of the Covenant. God sent Moses to Egypt to deliver Israel from 400 years of enslavement. Through Moses and under

God's fiery judgments, Israel left Egypt and journeyed into the wilderness. Instructions from Mt. Sinai came in the third month of their first year out (Ex. 19:1). Moses delivered the Israelites out of the land of Egypt, but the real challenge was getting Egypt out of Israel. They were not simply being delivered *from* a place but *to* a place, and more specifically to *someone*. The bridal paradigm takes time. Sometimes the wilderness is a great place to work out bridal issues (Hos. 2:14).

It was a fearful beginning. The wrath of Egypt was on everyone's mind. "The LORD was going before them in a pillar of cloud by day to lead them on the way, and in a pillar of fire by night to give them light, that they might travel by day and by night. He did not take away the pillar of cloud by day, nor the pillar of fire by night, from before the people" (Ex. 13:21-22).

God had a unique perspective on the world. He was a night and day God, as was reinforced for the apostle John when he saw the accuser of the brethren (Rev 12:10). When the Egyptians prepared to attack, God, as might have been expected, moved the cloud to stand behind them and the Israelites, and kept the Egyptians from a nighttime attack. The cloud stayed night and day, and would lift off from over the tabernacle whenever it was time to move to a new location (Num. 9:21). It may also have been the case that Israel could travel at night if the cloud lifted at night. Whether a nighttime move ever occurred is unclear, but it was possible (Neh. 9:12). Supernatural fire could certainly make travel safe at night because the darkness and the light are alike to God (Ps. 139:12). Israel might have done more than sleep at night. One wonders if God would have made a move at night at least once to teach Israel something about His nature. A time was coming when God made it clear to David that He was a night and day God and had a 24/7 job for Israel.

Moses constructed the *tent of meeting*, or *tabernacle of testimony*, as it was also known, according to the pattern God gave him on the mountain. "Then you shall erect the tabernacle according to its plan which you have been shown in the mountain" (Ex. 26:30). The writer to the Hebrews noted that Moses saw a copy or shadow (Heb. 8:5), but the real tabernacle existed in heaven (Heb. 9:24). The apostle John would later see the original (Rev. 15:5).

The Ark of the Covenant where God was enthroned was the crowning feature of the tent.

> The cherubim shall have their wings spread upward, covering the mercy seat with their wings and facing one another; the faces of the cherubim are to be turned toward the mercy seat. You shall put the mercy seat on top of the ark, and in the ark you shall put the testimony which I will give to you." (Ex. 25:20-21)

Moses placed the Ten Commandments—what God called His testimony—in the Ark.

> So He declared to you His covenant which He commanded you to perform, *that is*, the Ten Commandments; and He wrote them on two tablets of stone. The LORD commanded me at that time to teach you statutes

and judgments, that you might perform
them in the land where you are going over
to possess it. (Deut. 4:13-14)

He also placed the book detailing all God's judgments
and statutes beside the Ark.

It came about, when Moses finished writing
the words of this law in a book until they
were complete, that Moses commanded the
Levites who carried the ark of the covenant of the LORD, saying, Take this book
of the law and place it beside the ark of the
covenant of the LORD your God, that it
may remain there as a witness against you.
(Deut. 31:24-26)

It was a witness for the people. Moses actually wrote
a song containing the judgments and statutes of God and
taught it to Israel. We might describe it as a singing testimony (Deut. 31:22). Apart from Miriam's celebration with
timbrel (Ex. 20:15) at the defeat of Pharaoh's army and
Moses' song, not much is said about the place and practice
of song in that day.

The statutes and judgments were given for life *with* God.
Israel had been delivered from Egypt but following the law
would bring them in*to* life with God. It was a two-step process that Israel was reluctant to follow. As the requirements
of God's laws became clearer, the clamor to return to Egypt
began to grow (Num. 14:3-4). Dedication is a key attribute

in life with God. This message will show up repeatedly, and David is offered as the divine example of dedication.

The Ark was placed in an inner tent—the Holy of Holies. It was separated from the outer tent by a veil which could only be accessed by the high priest (Ex. 26:33-36). For Moses, the closest object to the mercy seat on top of the Ark of the Covenant was the golden altar of incense. It stood immediately outside the veil of the Holy of Holies. When we understand incense as prayer, the close proximity makes perfect sense. God is listening for those who call upon His name.

The entire tent or tabernacle stood in the enclosed courtyard that was walled off with its own entrance (Ex. 27:9-18). The Levites camped around the courtyard to protect the people from inappropriate access (Num. 1:50-53), and the rest of the Israelite camp formed around the Levites. All the ritually unclean people could not even be in the camp, forced to stay outside until they were declared clean (Lev. 14:8, 15:11-15).

Access to the Ark of God's presence was separate and very limited. The high priest could only enter once a year to see the Ark (Lev. 16:29-34). He could not come whenever he wanted (Lev. 16:2). Aaron had to be ordained, purified, and carry sacrificial blood and incense, or he would die (Ex. 28:41-43; Lev. 16:12-16). The Levites were ordained and purified as well (Num. 8:19-22). If they handled the artifacts of the tent directly, they too would die. If the tent was to be moved, the priests had to perform the tear-down and set-up. The Levites could only carry the holy objects when properly covered, and weren't even allowed to look at those artifacts uncovered on pain of death (Num. 4:17-20, 18:3). And no foreigner or unclean person could ever approach.

The people assembled at the tent in the wilderness. They were commanded to go and seek the Lord at the place He would choose when they moved into the Promised Land (Deut. 12:5). But they could only come to the doorpost of the tent (Lev. 8:3-4), and they had to be clean. Inappropriate approach to God or His holy things resulted in death. In spite of these dangers, all the young men were expected to appear before the Lord three times a year (Ex. 34:23). It is hard to see a Bridegroom God who desires intimacy at this stage in history.

Some of the Levites, along with Dathan and other leaders—men of renown—rose up to oppose Moses and Aaron (Num. 16:1-3) with a clear demand: the whole congregation was holy and consequently should have a voice in governing. It was a test of God's leadership, and He reacted swiftly. The conspirators perished as the earth swallowed them up and a plague was released. The people became frantic. "Then the sons of Israel spoke to Moses, saying, Behold, we perish, we are dying, we are all dying! Everyone who comes near, who comes near to the tabernacle of the LORD, must die. Are we to perish completely?" (Num. 17:12-13). God does not change (Mal. 3:6). He possesses the same nature in John's revelation as He does in Moses's time.

Commanded or not, Israel's desire to draw near just wasn't there. It is not hard to understand why the people wanted to return to Egypt. Life back in Egypt seemed much easier than trying to get close *to* God. Thankfully, God did not listen to their cry to return. As it turned out, there was more going on behind the scenes.

The prophets later revealed that all through the desert wanderings, the people of Israel were actually unfaithful and immoral. They claimed allegiance to the Lord in public (Ex. 19:8) and would clamor to God about His treatment of them as if they were innocent. However, the truth was quite different. They followed a host of other gods on the side. The prophet Amos commented on God's behalf: "Did you present Me with sacrifices and grain offerings in the wilderness for forty years, O house of Israel? You also carried along Sikkuth your king and Kiyyun, your images, the star of your gods which you made for yourselves" (Amos 5:25-26). God saw the reality and through Jeremiah shared His heart: "Go and proclaim in the ears of Jerusalem, saying, 'Thus says the LORD, I remember concerning you the devotion of your youth, The love of your betrothals, Your following after Me in the wilderness, Through a land not sown'" (Jer. 2:2-3). God's memory of events wasn't fuzzy. He chose to remember their devotion. As a Bridegroom God, He would contend with the people and does so even today. He did not walk away (though no one would have blamed Him if He had). He had abundant grounds for divorce.

God is holy (Lev. 11:45). His isolation in the tent clearly reflected this aspect of His nature. However, He was no less the Bridegroom God even if this attribute was not understood at this point in history. It is impossible to have a relationship without an exposed heart. Relationships are inherently risky for this reason. The tent might also have provided God with a measure of emotional separation from a continually wayward and stiff-necked people who had to be kept at arm's length until her heart changed. God gave this confession to Jeremiah.

Oh that my head were waters And my eyes a fountain of tears, That I might weep day and night For the slain of the daughter of my people! Oh that I had in the desert A wayfarers' lodging place; That I might leave my people And go from them! For all of them are adulterers, An assembly of treacherous men. "They bend their tongue *like* their bow; Lies and not truth prevail in the land; For they proceed from evil to evil, And they do not know Me," declares the LORD. (Jer. 9:1-3)

During the wilderness wanderings, God was not uninvolved. He took care of Israel. The cloud protected them when the enemy approached. He brought water out of the rock and manna from the sky. Their clothes did not wear out. But He also protected His heart as He watched for the movement of His people's heart! It didn't move much. Their behavior was unchanged, and eventually the adults who had come out of Egypt remained unfaithful. They did not pursue the Lord and died without seeing the Promised Land. Once again we see that the challenge for the bride in Revelation is the same as the challenge was for Israel. Heart driven devotion is key.

Unlike Aaron, the Levites, other leaders, and the people, Moses had extraordinary access to the presence of the Lord. He met with Him *face to face*. "Now when Moses went into the tent of meeting to speak with Him, he heard His voice coming from above the mercy seat on the ark of the testimony: from between the two cherubim, so He spoke to him" (Num. 7:89). The operation of the tent of meeting did not function like natural laws did. There were exceptions. His opponents considered themselves to be no different than Moses and expected similar treatment, and as a result, they died or were disciplined.

Why was Moses different? "Thus the LORD used to speak to Moses face to face, just as a man speaks to his friend" (Ex. 33:11). Moses was a friend of God. Undoubtedly, Moses placed the book of the law where he could meditate on God's words—in God's presence and before His face (Deut. 31:26). It was a witness for all of Israel, but most weren't watching. They should have been asking the critical question, "Why Moses?" Moses wasn't taking privilege upon himself. God was giving it.

Moses was humble, faithful, and desired above all else the presence of God. He did not wish to be sent on any mission with Israel or even to move about unless God was with them. Moses, having been schooled in all the learning of the Egyptians, was a man of power in word and deed (Acts 7:22). At age forty, he set out to help Israel. His first attempt ended in failure. After escaping from Egypt to avoid his murder conviction, he spent forty years in the wilderness. At the age of eighty, he told God, "Please, Lord, I have never been eloquent, neither recently nor in time past, nor since You have spoken to Your servant; for I am slow of speech and slow of tongue" (Ex. 4:10). It is difficult to imagine he was the same man. After this forty-year wait and the adversity of desert life, the word of the Lord came to Moses; and he was indeed sent to help his people. But he had become a very different man.

When Aaron and Miriam opposed Moses, God intervened and provided this revelation:

> He said, Hear now My words: If there is
> a prophet among you, I, the LORD, shall
> make Myself known to him in a vision. I
> shall speak with him in a dream. Not so,
> with My servant Moses, He is faithful in
> all My household; With him I speak mouth
> to mouth, Even openly, and not in dark
> sayings, And he beholds the form of the
> LORD. Why then were you not afraid To
> speak against My servant, against Moses?
> (Num. 12:6-8)

God's bridegroom heart is being expressed. It can be argued that Moses was operating in the office of leader and, as a result, had unusual access and support in his role. While this is true, it isn't the complete story. Being king of Israel was not a guarantee of friendship with God, as Saul the first king of Israel discovered. Only the inner circle of close friend(s) experience this full dimension of God. And outside of this circle, clarity and understanding begin to diminish incrementally until the fool can exclaim with great confidence, "There is no God" (Ps. 14:1).

Moses was dedicated but did not want to robotically follow God's instructions alone. "Now therefore, I pray You, if I have found favor in Your sight, let me know Your ways that I may know You, so that I may find favor in Your sight" (Ex. 33:13). This was not a cry to better understand God's instructions or to receive more instruction. The instructions he received were very detailed. Moses wanted to know God. Moses went further and asked God to show him His glory. This is relational dialogue and best understood within the bridal paradigm. God said yes, but gave Moses something unexpected: "And He said, 'I Myself will make all My goodness pass before you, and will proclaim the name of the LORD before you; and I will be gracious to whom I will be gracious, and will show compassion on whom I will show compassion'" (Ex. 33:19). God made all His goodness, rather than all His instructions, pass before Moses. This is the bedrock of God's being. He is good and actually desires to make His name known and reveal Himself. The contrast between the Moses' access to God and the access of everyone else is stunning.

Moses had failure in his life with consequences (Num. 20:2). Though he loved the testimonies of God, he didn't follow at least one instruction (Num. 20:11-12). In the grace of God, it did not have a lasting effect on his relationship with God. He was disciplined, but the earth did not swallow him up as it had done for Dathan. We are not given Moses' confession, but it is clear Moses did not become despondent or check out emotionally with a sense of shame. He asked God to change the outcome, and he likely did this repeatedly. God finally commanded Moses to speak no more of it. Moses continued to speak face to face with God through the rest of his days. Clearly, he had been forgiven, and clearly, he went forward with the Lord.

Moses fasted. They were supernatural fasts. No one can live without water for forty days without divine help. But fasting was part of the relationship (Deut. 9:18). "For I was afraid of the anger and hot displeasure with which the LORD was wrathful against you in order to destroy you, but the LORD listened to me that time also" (Deut. 9:19). He interceded—and not just once. Apart from the intercession of Moses, Israel would have been destroyed. Eventually the adults perished in the wilderness, but the children lived and went in to possess the Promised Land. Prayer with fasting is no small thing (Matt 17:21).

Moses wanted to preserve Israel. He wanted the people to flourish and draw near. He, himself, did not wish to be exceptional. "But Moses said to him, 'Are you jealous for my sake? Would that all the LORD'S people were prophets, that the LORD would put His Spirit upon them!'" (Num. 11:29). (Translation: "I wish all God's people had a growing revelation *of* and desire *for* God like I do.")

> Then Moses went up with Aaron, Nadab and Abihu, and seventy of the elders of Israel, and they saw the God of Israel; and under His feet there appeared to be a pavement of sapphire, as clear as the sky itself. Yet He did not stretch out His hand against the nobles of the sons of Israel; and they saw God, and they ate and drank. (Ex. 24:9-11)

The fellowship and friendship on the pavement of sapphire is amazing. And they didn't die. The elders received a taste; however, they didn't continue to press in.

God gave great revelation to Moses. He wrote most of the first five books of the Bible—God's commandments, statutes, and judgments, His testimony (Ex. 25:16)—with perhaps a small amount of editorial help from Joshua, his successor. Moses provided instruction and an example for those who marveled at his own exceptional access and were also moving from Egypt and drawing close to God. He even taught Israel a song extoling God's virtues and reminding them of His powerful promises and judgments. Exceptional access was possible, but perhaps Moses was just that, an exception, and dinner with God was a chance occurrence. The curious must read on.

Chapter Five

AARON AND THE TENT— *SHARATH*ING WITH GOD

A aron went through the ordination and purification process so he could minister to the Lord in the holy place. Moses had special vestments made for Aaron (Ex. 28:31) which he would wear whenever he entered the holy place to minister to the Lord. "They shall be on Aaron and on his sons when they enter the tent of meeting, or when they approach the altar to minister in the holy place, so that they do not incur guilt and die. It shall be a statute forever to him and to his descendants after him" (Ex. 28:43). The Hebrew word *Sharath*, translated here as *minister,* has an important history and a significant future. The word is first used with Joseph some 430 years before Israel's desert wanderings, and the word's history should be considered before moving on with Aaron.

Joseph, Jacob's beloved son, was sold into slavery as a teenager by his jealous brothers for twenty shekels of silver. He was taken to Egypt by Ishmaelite slave traders, who in turn sold him to Potiphar, an Egyptian officer who was the captain of Pharaoh's bodyguard. The Lord was with Joseph and prospered him in everything he did (Gen. 39:2-4).

Potiphar took note and made Joseph his personal servant—literally, the one who *sharath*s. He was so impressed with Joseph and his faithful and humble service that he left everything he owned in Joseph's care. Potiphar's only concern was feeding himself. You can almost feel Potiphar's joy and satisfaction at this fortuitous turn of events in his house.

But Joseph's favor with Potiphar didn't last. He was wrongly accused of molesting Potiphar's wayward wife and was thrown into prison. However, the hand of the Lord continued to be with Joseph. The chief jailer put Joseph in charge of all the prisoners (Gen. 39:21-23). He stopped supervising Joseph altogether because Joseph's *service* (*sharath*) was delightful and satisfying. His experience was like Potiphar's: His burden had been lifted, and he could attend to other things without a care.

It is not hard to detect the sense of satisfaction and delight that both Potiphar and the jailer had for Joseph's service. He was completely trustworthy, faithful even under great personal distress, and they were relieved to be able to turn responsibilities over to him. Joseph could have asked for anything. If it was within the power of these men, he would have had his requests.

It is true that Joseph's brothers had conspired together to sell him into slavery. However, the reality was that God had sent Joseph to Egypt to prepare for a devastating famine and save Israel. Many years later, Joseph would give his brothers his revised perspective. Joseph went from being a favored son with a many-colored coat and an attitude to being a servant who learned to *sharath*. This word does not appear in the dialogue with Pharaoh concerning his disturbing dreams, but the experience is the same. Pharaoh left everything in

Joseph's charge, as had the jailor and Potiphar. He became second in command next to Pharaoh. It was a remarkable transition for the one who had learned to *sharath*.

A later example of one who learns how to sharath is Aaron. In the early days of the tent of meeting, Aaron may well have needed to set his heart to learn how to *sharath*—moving in joyful service of His God. It might not have come naturally over time without setting his heart to it. He stepped out of his personal disappointment and distress to be pleasing in his *sharath* of the Lord.

The circumstances for both Joseph and Aaron were difficult. Aaron had to learn and master a whole new set of instructions around the operation of the tent of meeting. Two of his sons died when they approached the Lord inappropriately; and undoubtedly, Aaron's memory of the golden calf affair when he blessed Israel's scandalous sin (Ex. 32:4-6) was in the back of his mind. Aaron must have wondered why God wanted his *sharath at all*. He may have felt ashamed, unworthy, and at the same time angry and grieved over the loss of his sons. Likewise, Joseph must have felt deceived and unwanted as a result of his brothers' betrayal. Both Aaron and Joseph had a choice in how they responded to their circumstances.

Aaron entered into God's personal service. God did provide Aaron with help. "Bring the tribe of Levi near and set them before Aaron the priest that they may serve him. They shall perform the duties for him and for the whole congregation before the tent of meeting, to do the service of the tabernacle" (Num. 3:6-7). The Levites were asked to enter into personal service, and initially the object of *sharath* was Aaron and his sons. Not all the Levites liked this leadership arrangement, as noted in the previous chapter. Moses added a correction into the conversation on leadership.

> Is it not enough for you that the God of Israel has separated you from the *rest* of the congregation of Israel, to bring you near to Himself, to do the service of the tabernacle of the LORD, and to stand before the congregation to minister to them and that He has brought you near, *Korah*, and all your brothers, sons of Levi, with you? And are you seeking for the priesthood also? (Num. 16:9-10)

It was a privilege to *sharath*, not a burden to bear. The Levites were not only *sharath*ing Aaron, but the congregation and the tabernacle as well. Their role had significance in God's eyes, but required humility. Korah and others thought differently. Their choice worked out badly.

Later, the Levites were called to carry the Ark of the Covenant, stand before the Lord to *sharath* Him, and then turn to bless the congregation (Deut. 10:8). Humility won out. Serving one another led to serving the Lord. In addition, it would seem there was a connection between *sharath*ing the Lord and distributing a blessing. Joseph, likewise, released a blessing in the earth, as did Abraham. Pharaoh was only interested in his own realm. The work of Joseph kept the known world alive. "*The people of* all the earth came to Egypt to buy grain from Joseph, because the famine was severe in all the earth" (Gen. 41:57). God did not let Korah and company change His plans. The call to *sharath* didn't sit well with some. Perspective, humility and a devoted heart had a lot to do with the ability to *sharath*.

Aaron and his descendants were the only ones allowed to lay incense before the Lord. "…as a reminder to the sons of Israel that no layman who is not of the descendants of Aaron should come near to burn incense before the LORD; so that he will not become like Korah and his company—just as the LORD had spoken to him through Moses" (Num. 16:40). At the time, only Aaron was permitted to perform the ministry of incense. When Korah's disobedience led to the release of a plague, it was incense that God called Aaron to use to stop it.(Num. 16:46). Offering incense was not just a privilege. It stopped the plague, turning the heart of God. The saints lived for another day.

Although access was restricted, the tent of meeting became an important place to gain wisdom and settle disputes. It was at the tent where Aaron's rod bloomed in support of God's call on the house of Levi (Num. 17:8). Moses went further in his instructions. "Then the priests, the sons of Levi, shall come near, for the LORD your God has chosen them to serve Him and to bless in the name of the LORD; and every dispute and every assault shall be settled by them" (Deut. 21:5). They were chosen to *sharath* and bless, and consequently, God would give them governmental wisdom to solve every dispute. "If any case is too difficult for you to decide, between one kind of homicide or another, between one kind of lawsuit or another, and between one kind of assault or another, being cases of dispute in your courts, then you shall arise and go up to the place which the LORD your God chooses" (Deut. 17:8).

For the really hard cases, they had to travel to a place of the Lord's choosing to hear from Him. "The man who acts presumptuously by not listening to the priest who stands there to serve the LORD your God, nor to the judge, that man shall die; thus you shall purge the evil from Israel" (Deut. 17:12). The Levitical priests had governmental responsibility. The priest who *sharath*ed the Lord made the final determination. They were the end of the line of appeals.

Hopefully, the high priest *sharath*ing the Lord at that time would render a decision based on an existing statute. The Ten Commandments and the book of the law were placed conspicuously before the mercy seat under the wings of the cherubim as a witness or testimony to the people and as a resource. Those words expressed God's thoughts and intentions. If the decision went beyond what was known, the priest would receive the necessary wisdom from the one (God) he *sharath*ed.

In Moses' day, the case of the daughters of Zelophehad exemplified the process (Num. 27:1-2). Their father had died in the wilderness, and he left no sons but only daughters. The question of inheritance rights was brought before Moses and Eleazar the priest, at which time the Lord spoke to Moses and provided a new statute to be applied going forward for similar cases.

God called Aaron and then the Levites to *sharath* Him. He taught them His statutes and judgments and supported them in their application of His words. When necessary, He gave them added revelation to meet the need. The glue to make it work appeared to be the heart to *sharath*!

The word appeared next in relation to Joshua. He was described as Moses' servant (Ex. 24:13). Joshua succeeded

Moses, and Israel began the conquest of the Promised Land. God made a startling statement to Joshua: "No man will be able to stand before you all the days of your life. Just as I have been with Moses, I will be with you; I will not fail you or forsake you" (Josh. 1:5). Joshua, like Moses, would have exceptional access. God would not speak to him in dark sayings, but rather face to face. Would he learn to *sharath* the Lord?

Chapter Six

THE QUIET YEARS

L ike Moses, Joseph, and Aaron, Joshua had a time of
training and dedication. While the tabernacle was
being constructed, Moses met with the Lord in a simple tent
he had pitched outside the camp. "When Moses returned to
the camp, his *servant* Joshua, the son of Nun, a young man,
would not depart from the tent" (Ex. 33:11). Joshua was
described as Moses' servant (Ex.24:13), one who *sharath*s
his master— causing the delightful and satisfying experience
of his master. Joshua most likely maintained this practice
even after the tabernacle was completed and God's meeting
tent shifted back into the midst of the Israelite camp. This
would be his practice for forty years. His early *sharath*ing
of Moses prepared him to serve the Lord as Israel took the
Promised Land.

Joshua was a family man, military leader, and an under-
study to Moses. He had plenty to do, but his priority was
around the tent of meeting. It might appear to have been
inconvenient, but it was not a conflict of interest: His time
was the Lord's and Joshua went out to do life as needed.
He was fully spiritual and fully natural. He was commis-
sioned to spy out the land. When the Amalekites attacked

(Ex. 17:13), Joshua led the army to victory. Later in his life, Joshua would challenge the people on their devotion to God. They needed to choose which god they would serve. For Joshua and his family, the choice was obvious: They would follow the Lord (Josh. 24:14-15).

On the eve of going into Jericho, God spoke to Joshua. Three times He told Joshua to be strong and courageous. He was leaving the desert life where God had provided their food, shelter and clothing. The Israelites had not gone this way before (Josh. 3:4). God instructed Joshua: "This book of the law shall not depart from your mouth, but you shall meditate on it day and night, so that you may be careful to do according to all that is written in it; for then you will make your way prosperous, and then you will have success" (Josh. 1:8). When Moses had finished writing the book of the law, he placed it beside the Ark of the Covenant in the tent of meeting. There may have been additional copies made, but the original had been completed shortly before Moses went to be with the Lord. And Joshua put the finishing touches on it. God appeared to be referencing the copy in His tent. Joshua, who had exceptional access like Moses, could come before the Lord in the tent to study day and night.

Joshua had not been commanded to stay by the tent in the early days. It appeared to be his voluntary practice. Now, the Lord commanded night and day meditation. The testimonies of God should be reviewed, considered, and thoroughly digested day and night and declared verbally. The lamp in the Holy Place would make nighttime study quite feasible. God promised a result for this tabernacle-driven lifestyle: Joshua would prosper and have success. God wanted His book to be read before Him night and day. He may well have added verbal commentary as Joshua read.

Joshua, like Moses, experienced failure. The Gibeonites gave a credible but duplicitous story. They alleged that they were not from the nations in the Promised Land that God intended to forcefully remove but had come a long distance because of the fame of the Lord. The Israelite leaders bought the tale. It was so credible that Joshua did not take it before the Lord (Josh. 9:14). There were consequences to this. Joshua and the army were forced to take military action to defend Gibeon. God redeemed the situation and used it for His purposes, but the Gibeonites were able to stay in the land. They were cursed and became "hewers of wood and drawers of water for the house of my God" (Josh. 9:23). Ironically, the pagan Gibeonites helped keep sacrifices moving along even when the Ark of the Covenant was no longer in Moses' tent of meeting in the time of Saul. Religious activity without relationship can carry on for a long time.

During Joshua's early days, a controversy broke out between the tribes of Israel around creating a copy of the altar. "Therefore we said, 'It shall also come about if they say this to us or to our generations in time to come, then we shall say, See the copy of the altar of the LORD which our fathers made, not for burnt offering or for sacrifice; rather it is a witness between us and you'" (Josh. 22:28). Israel almost went to war with the two and one-half Transjordan tribes. They were afraid their brothers had created a copy of the brazen altar to pursue God on their own, away from the place God would choose, and thus bring God's condemnation upon the entire nation. Once they were convinced the altar was going to be a witness rather than a place for burnt offerings, war was averted. In the Septuagint (LXX), the Greek translation of the Hebrew Old Testament created around 250 BC, the word *marturion* (testimony) was used. It was the same word the apostle John would later use in the New Testament. There would be only one official place for sacrifice, but testimonies to what God had done could in theory exist in multiple locations. Perhaps Malachi many years later tapped into this idea of multiple testimonies (Mal. 1:11). This will be considered further in Chapter Fourteen.

Israel served the LORD all the days of Joshua and all the days of the elders who survived Joshua (Josh. 24:31). Joshua told the people to put away their gods they had served in Egypt and in their wilderness wandering. This, evidently, Israel did not do. Religious life continued to decline. *Sharath* does not appear again until the days of Samuel.

The Ark was only mentioned once in the book of Judges. A Levite traveling through Benjamin with his concubine and servant came to Gibeah in the evening. An old man coming in from the field saw them sitting in the town square, and offered the Levite hospitality and a place to stay. However, the men of the town rose up. They intended to sexually abuse the Levite. This breach of hospitality led to the brutal death of the Levite's concubine, and the Levite called all Israel to consider the actions of Gibeah and respond. Israel was shocked, but the sons of Benjamin would not punish the men of Gibeah. War quickly followed.

Israel went up to Bethel to inquire of God and receive His battle plans (Judg. 20:18). At that time the Ark of the Covenant was there. Since it was mobile, it could be moved for special occasions. Although it is not mentioned, the tent and the rest of the tent of meeting artifacts most likely stayed behind in Shiloh. This would allow the daily sacrificial requirements to be fulfilled. The book of Judges represents a particularly dark time for Israel—a time of repeated national failure and deliverance—everyone did what was right in their own eyes (Judg. 17:6). Into this generally low state of affairs, Samuel appeared; and he, like Moses, was no ordinary child.

Samuel's mother was barren. It was a painful time for Hannah. She was one of two wives and her rival, Peninnah, had success in bearing children and taunted her. Their husband, Elkanah, loved Hannah, but she remained barren. Each year the family would go to Shiloh to worship and sacrifice. "Then Hannah rose after eating and drinking in Shiloh. Now Eli the priest was sitting on the seat by the doorpost of the temple of the LORD" (1 Sam. 1:9). She came to the door of the tent or structure that housed the Ark as Israel was instructed to do (Ex. 29:42-43), and Hannah made her appeal to God.

In great bitterness, she poured out her heart to God. She asked for a son and promised he would grow up as a Nazirite and be given to the Lord. The Lord listened to Hannah's petition and gave her a son. Once he was weaned, she brought him to Shiloh to *sharath* the Lord. God did not let the sacrifice go unnoticed. He gave Hannah five more children. *Sharath* has a sacrificial element too!

A man of God came to Eli, the priest at Shiloh, and pronounced judgment on his house. God rebuked Eli for allowing his sons to profane God's things, and God promised to raise up a faithful priest to replace his family (1 Sam. 2:35-36). Two verses later, Samuel entered Eli's life. Samuel was probably three to five years of age when Hannah weaned him (1 Sam. 1:22) and presented him to Eli, the priest at Shiloh.

"Then Elkanah went to his home at Ramah. But the boy ministered to the LORD before Eli the priest" (1 Sam. 2:11). Samuel as a young boy *sharath*ed the Lord. Aaron *sharath*ed the Lord in the Holy Place (Ex. 28:41-43). The Levites *sharath*ed Aaron (Num. 3:6), and then the Levites *sharath*ed the Lord in all the operation of the tent of meeting (Deut. 10:8) and *sharath*ed the congregation (Num. 16:9). Samuel was now brought near to *sharath* the Lord.

"Now the boy Samuel was ministering to the LORD before Eli. And word from the LORD was rare in those days, visions were infrequent" (1 Sam. 3:1). The juxtaposition of *sharath*ing the Lord to the presence (absence) of words and visions is fascinating. No *sharath*ing, no visions!

> It happened at that time as Eli was lying down in his place (now his eyesight had begun to grow dim, and he could not see well), and the lamp of God had not yet gone out, and Samuel was lying down in the temple of the LORD where the ark of God was, that the LORD called Samuel; and he said, "Here I am". (1 Sam. 3:2-4)

It appears that Samuel slept near the Ark of the Covenant or at least in close proximity—perhaps in the Holy Place where the lamp of God was located. The actual set-up of the temple in Shiloh is not known. That he would actually sleep in the temple where the Ark was located and do so apart from ordination requirements (Lev. 8:35) is astonishing. The tent of meeting practice had definitely changed since the days of Moses.

Samuel had not experienced the audible voice of the Lord before, and when the Lord spoke, Samuel thought Eli was calling him. Samuel went to Eli to hear what his master required. Eli had not called him, so he sent Samuel back to bed. After the second occurrence, Eli caught on to what was happening. He coached Samuel to address the Lord when the voice came again. Samuel was ready. When God spoke, Samuel responded as Eli directed. God brought a heavy word of judgment upon Eli's house, and Samuel was afraid to report those words to Eli.

Josephus, a Jewish historian at the time of the first century AD Roman invasion, believed Samuel was perhaps twelve when he first heard the Word of the Lord (NIV Study Bible, notes on 1 Sam. 3:1). Samuel, like Moses, Aaron, and Joshua, had extraordinary access to God:

> Thus Samuel grew and the LORD was with him and let none of his words fail. All Israel from Dan even to Beersheba knew that Samuel was confirmed as a prophet of the LORD. And the LORD appeared again at Shiloh, because the LORD revealed Himself to Samuel at Shiloh by the word of the LORD. (1 Sam. 3:19-21)

Like Moses (Ex. 33:17), Samuel had favor. Assuming he arrived to minister before the age of five and that Josephus had access to good information, Samuel had had seven-plus years or longer to build intimacy with the Lord; and then the word of the Lord came. Delay was at work. We only have record of family contact when Samuel's mother would come to visit once a year with a new robe. It must have been distressing for Samuel to grow up without parents, family, or like-minded friends when they didn't live that far away. Samuel had a unique place in God's heart, as evidenced by God expressing His heart to him when Israel first clamored for a king: "Like all the deeds which they have done since the day that I brought them up from Egypt even to this day—in that they have forsaken Me and served other gods—so they are doing to you also" (1 Sam. 8:8). God shared intimate details and emotion with Samuel.

Israel's desire for a king—a human intermediary, even if it was a divinely appointed one—was not what God wanted. Samuel, the friend of God, was distressed by Israel's request. Samuel took the rejection personally, and God saw it. Such was their friendship. God was clearly pleased by Samuel's *sharath*ing, just as Potiphar and the jailor and later Pharaoh were pleased with Joseph. God never desired a human intermediary. He wanted face-to-face contact; exceptional access has always been God's plan for His people. Unfortunately, this need for a human intermediary has plagued the saints ever since. "Now Samuel judged Israel all the days of his life. He went on circuit annually to Bethel and Gilgal and Mizpah judging Israel in all these places. Then his return was to Ramah, for his house was there, and there he judged Israel; and he built there an altar to the LORD" (1 Sam. 7:15-17). Samuel was not reproached for building a copy of the altar to offer burnt offerings as the two and one-half Transjordan tribes had been. It wasn't a testimony or witness. He was presumably offering sacrifice to the Lord. The altar wasn't in Shiloh, Nob, or Gibeon, where the tent of meeting was later located.

Shiloh appeared to have been the main home for the tent of meeting up until the time the Philistines overran Israel in battle and captured the Ark. God Himself would destroy Shiloh as prophesied through the man of God and executed, most likely, through the hands of the Philistines (Jer. 7:12). Eli, Samuel's mentor, died when he heard the bad news, and his daughter-in-law went into labor. As she was dying, she named her son Ichabod, meaning *the glory has departed*. The tent of meeting, what was left, moved to Nob, but the Ark took a different path. The Ark stayed in the Philistine territory for seven months, but their victory trophy became a terrible burden.

> They sent therefore and gathered all the lords of the Philistines and said, Send away the ark of the God of Israel, and let it return to its own place, so that it will not kill us and our people. For there was a deadly confusion throughout the city; the hand of God was very heavy there. (1 Sam. 5:11)

Mismanagement of the presence of God had international consequences. It affected the Philistine cities and their operation. The impact of the deadly confusion was throughout the city. The people became unruly and distressed. Good government is challenging at the best of times, but under this circumstance, it was impossible. The negative impact of the Ark offered in this account is significant.

Inappropriate worship impacts a city! David would shortly provide a different example, and the prophets would later affirm what David did.

The Ark was sent back to the men of Beth-shemesh, who were no wiser than the Philistines. They were grateful to see the Ark, but it was a novelty—a good luck charm or rabbit's foot—to them. God struck down 50,000 who irreverently looked into the Ark.

The Ark was quickly sent away to Kiriath-jearim. It was clearly an unmanageable asset, talisman or not.

> And the men of Kiriath-jearim came and took the ark of the LORD and brought it into the house of Abinadab on the hill, and consecrated Eleazar his son to keep the ark of the LORD. From the day that the ark remained at Kiriath-jearim, the time was long, for it was twenty years; and all the house of Israel lamented after the LORD. (1 Sam. 7:1-2)

No attempt was made to restore the Ark to Moses' tent of meeting. It is not clear if Eleazar was a descendant of Aaron. Israel lamented but was willing to have the Ark hidden away for twenty years at Abinadab's home. If Samuel had some thoughts on the matter, they are not recorded.

Aside from his early years, there is little said in the Scriptures about how and when Samuel continued to sharath the Lord.. The context for *sharath*ing for Aaron and the Levites was the tent of meeting and all its operation and maintenance. By the time of Samuel, a subtle shift was apparently underway. The Bridegroom God was again making exceptions and was beginning to change what it meant to *sharath*. It was no longer exclusively the support of the sacrificial system that priests and Levities were called to do. It was becoming more about God and the pleasure He experienced at the hands of His servants.

There is no mention of Samuel ever attempting to bring the Ark to himself at Ramah. He grew up sleeping by or near the Ark. He continued to hear God's voice throughout his ministry. The people revered Samuel as a man of God, a prophet, priest, and seer. It is hard to imagine Samuel not taking action to restore the Ark to the tent of meeting when it was at Nob and later Gibeon. His actions appear mysterious. The nature of *sharath*ing was further changing. Up to this point in time, the *sharath* of the Lord had been limited to leaders. Would it ever go beyond and touch the people at large? Time would tell.

Chapter Seven

THE HEART OF A KING

E ven though Samuel was a great leader, the Israelites wanted a king. God was king, but Israel coveted a human king like other countries. God warned them through Samuel that a king would appoint commanders and servants from their sons and daughters to plow and reap his fields. A king would need the large share of finances to sustain himself and his servants. And he would take for his work the best of the young men (1 Sam. 8:12-16). It was a warning Israel refused to heed.

> When you saw that Nahash the king of the sons of Ammon came against you, you said to me, 'No, but a king shall reign over us,' although the LORD your God was your king. Now therefore, here is the king whom you have chosen, whom you have asked for, and behold, the LORD has set a king over you. If you will fear the LORD and serve Him, and listen to His voice and not rebel against the command of the LORD, then both you and also the king who reigns over

you will follow the LORD your God. (1
Sam. 12:12-14)

The people were given a mirror: if they obeyed the voice
of the Lord, then both they and their king would follow the
Lord. If you want to know how a country and its people
are doing, look at its king's actions. God can always sover-
eignly break in—and did in several instances—but this is the
stated pattern and has application beyond Israel. King and
people look alike. God gave Israel a man after the heart of
the people. Samuel anointed Saul at Mizpah.

Saul was a man of stature. He stood head and shoulders
over his brethren and looked like he would be a formidable
leader and commander (1 Sam. 10:23). To the human eye, he
fit the role of a king to perfection. Yet something was wrong
from the very beginning. God spoke to the nation of Israel
when they came out of Egypt. Out of all the nations of the
earth, God chose Israel to be His possession—a holy nation
of priests (Ex. 19:3-6). God chose Israel to have national
prominence and visibility before the nations. They were a
chosen vessel to bring salvation to the earth (Isa. 26:18).
Samuel gathered the people to present Saul to them, but
he could not be found. "Therefore they inquired further of
the LORD, 'Has the man come here yet?' So the LORD
said, 'Behold, he is hiding himself by the baggage'" (1 Sam.
10:22). Israel did not wish to walk in its God-given role, and
neither did its new king.

The account of the Mizpah gathering (1 Sam. 10:17)
follows the account of the return of the Ark from storage in
Abinadab's home (1 Sam. 7:1). Although the Ark is not mentioned in connection with the coronation of Saul at Mizpah,

54

it is reasonable to assume that the Ark was brought from Abinadab's home and then returned afterward. The twenty-year period at Abinadab's home may reflect the elapsed time until the Mizpah gathering.

The Chronicler indicates that the Ark was of no interest during Saul's reign (1 Chron. 13:3). He reigned for thirty-two years. David succeeded Saul as king and reigned in Hebron for seven years before taking Jerusalem permanently and recovering the Ark from Abinadab's house. The time between the return of the Ark from Philistine territory and the coronation of Saul is not clear, but it may be the twenty years mentioned previously. If that was the case, the Ark was not part of the mainstream for at least fifty-nine years: twenty years from the return of the Ark to the Mizpah gathering, thirty-two years from the reign of Saul to the time of David, and seven years until Jerusalem was retaken.

Saul appeared to be confused about God's things. He needed direction as he prepared for war with the Philistines, and he commanded Ahijah the priest to bring him the Ark of God (1 Sam. 14:18-19). It is clear from the context that what he really wanted was the breastpiece/ephod. Aaron was commanded to carry the names of the sons of Israel in the breastpiece of judgment over his heart when he entered the Holy Place (Ex. 28:29). The Urim and the Thummim were stored in the breastpiece that was attached to the ephod (Lev. 8:8), and it was Ahijah's job to inquire for Saul by the judgment of the Urim before the LORD (Num. 27:21). Samuel or a later editor made no attempt to correct this passage to protect Saul's reputation.

The Chronicler recorded a meeting of David and Samuel during the time of Saul.

> Zechariah the son of Meshelemiah was
> gatekeeper of the entrance of the tent of
> meeting. All these who were chosen to be
> gatekeepers in the thresholds were 212.
> These were enrolled by genealogy in their
> villages, whom David and Samuel the seer
> appointed in their office of trust. So they
> and their sons had charge of the gates of the
> House of the Lord, even the house of the
> tent, as guards. (1 Chron. 9:21-23)

David had official responsibilities in Saul's government, so it was early in his relationship with Saul. Samuel and David worked out the gatekeeper schedule at the House of the Lord in Nob, but oddly there is no recorded mention of the Ark. Since David did not retrieve the Ark of the Covenant from Nob when he captured Jerusalem, it would seem the House of the Lord could function without the Lord of the house, who was enthroned upon the Ark. Religious practice hummed along nicely all on its own!

Saul's reign as king began to unravel. The Philistines gathered a sizeable army and came up against Saul. Israel was summoned to the battle, but they were hard pressed and began to hide themselves wherever they found shelter. Saul saw his troops melting away and could not wait as instructed. Samuel was coming to offer the burnt offering, and Saul had agreed to wait seven days for that event. When Samuel didn't arrive at the designated time, Saul decided to act on his own initiative. He offered the burnt offering, himself. Samuel arrived shortly thereafter. On the surface, Saul's actions don't appear out of line, but Saul's response and Samuel's commentary are telling. "I have not asked the favor of the LORD. So I forced myself and offered the burnt offering" (1 Sam. 13:12). Samuel recognized Saul's rationalization as disobedience. Consequently, Saul's kingdom would not endure, and God would now search for a man after His own heart.

Sometime later, Saul was given very specific instructions for going to battle against Amalek—Israel's ancient enemy. Again, Saul did not follow God's express instructions. Saul chose to rationalize what he obviously considered minor improvements to God's instructions. Rather than completely destroying Amalek—putting them under the ban—Saul let the king live and kept the choicest things for a sacrifice to the Lord at Gilgal. The Lord called it sin. Samuel called it sin. Saul's response gave further insight into his heart. He pleaded "I have sinned; *but* please honor me now before the elders of my people and before Israel, and go back with me, that I may worship the LORD your God" (1 Sam. 15:30). Saul was more interested in appearance—note, *my* people but *your* God—than having a broken heart. Samuel returned as requested but was grieved. He returned to his home in Ramah and did not see Saul again.

The Spirit of the Lord left Saul, and an evil spirit from the Lord terrorized him (1 Sam. 16:14). His dark days became more and more numerous. Once he determined that David was his replacement, he actively looked for ways to destroy him. And when David fled, Saul pursued. Those who innocently helped David became enemies of the state. Saul ordered the death of eighty priests in Nob because Ahimelech the priest unwittingly gave bread to David and his men who were fleeing (1 Sam. 21:2). Saul was unmoved by Ahimelech's account of the events.

Saul appears to be one who wanted instructions (as needed) but not relationship. Waiting on the Lord was not something he wanted to do. He was concerned about formal religious affairs and his appearance before men. Saul was impatient and disobedient, did not hold himself accountable for his actions, and was eventually removed by God. He was not like Moses, Joshua, Samuel, or even David. He is the antithesis of the godly leader, and as Samuel had warned, the people mirrored Saul's qualities. "But now your kingdom shall not endure. The LORD has sought out for Himself a man after His own heart, and the LORD has appointed him as ruler over His people, because you have not kept what the LORD commanded you" (1 Sam. 13:14). God announced His leadership qualification: it was all about the heart. The Bridegroom God had spoken.

In contrast to Saul, young David wasn't even a consideration in the selection process. He was not invited to join his older brothers in meeting with the prophet Samuel. David cared for the sheep and it was expected that whatever important deed Samuel required would be carried out by his older brothers. However, to Samuel's surprise, God rejected each one of David's brothers as a potential king. Samuel thought surely that Eliab, the oldest, was the one on God's heart (1 Sam. 16:6). God directed him to not look at the external appearance (1 Sam. 16:7), but to look at the heart. Jesse was commanded to bring in his youngest son. It was a God-ordained object lesson for Samuel and future generations.

The Spirit rushed upon David when he was anointed by Samuel (1 Sam. 16:13). David had an early burst of acclaim with the death of Goliath and with Philistine military defeats, but adversity and delay soon caught up with him. He fell out of favor with Saul and spent the next thirteen-plus years evading him and trying to stay alive. Saul recognized the threat David represented. None of Saul's sons could succeed him as king as long as David was alive. It is risky to shine too brightly before the king.

David lived in wilderness caves around Israel with a rough group of disgruntled men. He was constantly on the move, just barely staying ahead of Saul's army. Saul eventually died in battle and David was crowned king in Hebron. He reigned in Hebron for seven years and then retook Jerusalem, which became the capital of the united Israel. David's adversity training began to bear fruit.

Chapter Eight

DAVID

D avid was unlike Saul. His predecessor hid from his responsibilities, but David chose differently. Achish, the Philistine king, gave David and his men the town of Ziklag as a base of operations (1 Sam. 27:6). Saul had relentlessly searched for David and his men until they finally left Judah and came to Ziklag. They were mustered for battle by the Philistines and when they were away an Amalekite army raided Ziklag and carried off everything and everyone. When David and his men returned, there was outrage and near mutiny.

> Moreover David was greatly distressed because the people spoke of stoning him, for all the people were embittered, each one because of his sons and his daughters. But David strengthened himself in the LORD his God. Then David said to Abiathar the priest, the son of Ahimelech, "Please bring me the ephod." So Abiathar brought the ephod to David. David inquired of the LORD. (1 Sam. 30:6-8)

David chose to draw near to God and not flee or hide. God gave David what he needed, and he was able to recover everything that had been taken.

David did not want to leave God and the Ark of the Covenant tucked away in its obscure location at Abinadab's home (2 Sam. 6:4) in Baale-judah. He wanted to restore it to Israel's religious life. He tried to transport the Ark to Jerusalem on a cart, rather than having it hand-carried by Levites. This was a sensible approach. However, common sense only has value when God has not already spoken (Deut. 10:8). David gathered 30,000 chosen men of Israel to return the Ark amidst great celebration. Although well-intentioned, Uzzah died when he reached out to steady the Ark that was going to fall off the cart. God's action surprised and distressed David. He was angry but did his homework. The fear of the Lord gained a stronger hold of his heart that day, and in his next attempt he had the Levites carry the Ark to Jerusalem as prescribed. David's relationship with the Bridegroom God was growing. He was responsive to correction, and unlike his predecessor Saul, changed his methods to align with God.

Moving the Ark of the Covenant in an inappropriate manner was tragic, but it was not cold and calculated like the adultery with Bathsheba and murder of Uriah. When David was confronted in this next episode, he made no attempt to rationalize his behavior. He was deeply convicted, repented, and went forward with the Lord. Again, the broken-hearted response of David stands in sharp contrast to the *caught in the act* repentance of Saul. David was not concerned with his image. He poured out his heart instead. "Against You, You only, I have sinned and done what is evil in Your sight, So that You are justified when You speak And blameless when You judge" (Ps. 51:4). David's murderous actions are no different than Saul's. The two kings are not distinguishable in their depravity, but rather in their contrition and desire for restoration.

For David, God was approachable and not secluded. "One thing I have asked from the LORD, that I shall seek: That I may dwell in the House of the Lord all the days of my life, To behold the beauty of the LORD And to meditate in His temple" (Ps. 27:4). David was a *one thing* man. He wanted to dwell in God's presence—literally. He wanted to behold the beauty of God and meditate (investigate carefully and consider) in His presence. Intimacy was on his mind. Fervency and dedication were in his steps. David's testimony was deepening. He could be distressed and at times depressed, but never was he bored with God; being disengaged never seemed to be an issue for David.

David clearly expressed his heart. "When You said, Seek My face, my heart said to You, Your face, O LORD, I shall seek" (Ps. 27:8). Such was his obedience and devotion. Encounter, pursuit, intimacy, and friendship were on David's heart. He was forceful and resolute in his pursuit of the one He loved. As a young king, he hungered for the face of God. Religious observance or ritual practice were not drivers for David. Rather, he set his heart to passionately pursue God's face. He took the kingdom of God by storm.

"But as for me, I am like a green olive tree in the house of God; I trust in the lovingkindness of God forever and ever. I will give You thanks forever, because You have done *it*, And I will wait on Your name, for *it is* good, in the presence of Your godly ones" (Ps. 52:8-9). David compared himself to the green olive tree. He flourished in God's House. He would wait for God along with the other godly ones. Waiting is an action term. In Psalm 119:95, this term is used negatively but we sense the intensity of the action—the wicked lie in wait. Watchful scrutiny, alertness, and delay are all part of that negative image. Waiting on and for the Lord has the same intense attributes. Results will come but may be delayed. Waiting expects an outcome and engages, whether you are a bandit or lovesick worshiper. Waiting on and for God was David's desire. This was a key dimension of faith. Saul grew agitated in the wait. Not so with David.

> For zeal for Your house has consumed me,
> And the reproaches of those who reproach
> You have fallen on me. When I wept in my
> soul with fasting, It became my reproach.
> When I made sackcloth my clothing, I
> became a byword to them. Those who sit
> in the gate talk about me, And I *am* the song
> of the drunkards. But as for me, my prayer
> is to You, O LORD, at an acceptable time;
> O God, in the greatness of Your lovingk-
> indness, Answer me with Your saving truth.
> (Ps. 69:9-13)

David was zealous for the House of the Lord. It consumed him. He had to attend to many affairs of state and do life as needed, but his heart's true desire was to be in the Lord's presence. (Jesus would later quote David. Zeal for the House of the Lord consumed Him as well [John 2:17].) David had family, military, and governmental responsibilities;

obviously, he left the House of the Lord, God's House, to attend to these. He had integrity in his actions. He didn't neglect or slight his responsibilities, but his allegiance was clear. There were probably days when all he had time to do was run in and run out of the House of the Lord. Regardless, His house was always on David's mind.

David was consumed by his desire for God's House and bore reproach from family, friends, and foe alike because of it. David bore reproach because His God bore reproach. Samuel had a similar experience (1 Sam. 8:8). Weeping, fasting, and sackcloth were not unfamiliar to David (Ps. 69:10-11). He cared nothing for his reputation (Ps. 69:12) but trusted God to defend him. Most kings would be devoted to themselves—their kingdom, prosperity, and reputation. David was a very different king. He was a servant who served his God. "Let all who seek You rejoice and be glad in You; Let those who love Your salvation say continually, 'The LORD be magnified!'" (Ps. 40:16). It is not hard to see why God was so pleased with David's service!

David also had urgency. "How he swore to the LORD And vowed to the Mighty One of Jacob, Surely I will not enter my house, Nor lie on my bed; I will not give sleep to my eyes Or slumber to my eyelids, Until I find a place for the LORD, A dwelling place for the Mighty One of Jacob" (Ps. 132:2-5). David certainly took rest for himself, but his intensity and purpose were clear. The Spirit had rushed upon him as a young man. He had been given supernatural power to defeat Goliath and kill the bear and lion. His song was so anointed that he could minister to Saul when he was tormented by demons. He not only had a devotional and revelatory life, as evidenced in all the Psalms that bear his name, but he desperately wanted to dwell with God. David was one who had truly learned to sharath, to serve His God with great abandon and passion— a forerunner in the House of the Lord.

David could have been satisfied with a private devotional life or even a small group of friends who were as devoted as he was. However, he believed it was absolutely necessary to create an actual, corporate dwelling place in his community before the face of God, where he and other like-minded souls could gather before the Lord. Personal, private devotion was not enough. Neither could the Lord's house be a one-man show with spectators. It was truly corporate. He would even lay aside his kingly robe, take up his harp, and join the band (Ps. 108:2-3).

"Now behold, with great pains I have prepared for the House of the Lord 100,000 talents of gold and 1,000,000 talents of silver, and bronze and iron beyond weight, for they are in great quantity; also timber and stone I have prepared, and you may add to them" (1 Chron. 22:14). He gave extravagantly to God's House—in excess of $200 billion by today's accounting—based on just the gold and silver alone, and he expected to dwell before the Lord in His house. His time, treasure, and talent belonged to God. He was a restless First Commandment saint who wanted more and more of God.

> So David said to Michal, *It* was before the LORD, who chose me above your father and above all his house, to appoint me ruler over the people of the LORD, over Israel; therefore I will celebrate before the LORD.

> I will be more lightly esteemed than this and
> will be humble in my own eyes, but with the
> maids of whom you have spoken, with them
> I will be distinguished. (2 Sam. 6:21-22)

David was king, but like Moses he did not use his position to garner respect and accolades. He did not require special treatment. He was humble. He considered himself to be a poor man (Ps. 34:6). He did not refer to his substantial wealth but to the condition of his soul. He needed God. David experienced firsthand the intervention of God. The afflicted, the humble, and the poor could come to God's House and find help. God would break the cycle of poverty of soul and body. "For He has not despised nor abhorred the affliction of the afflicted; Nor has He hidden His face from him; But when he cried to Him for help, He heard … The afflicted will eat and be satisfied; Those who seek Him will praise the LORD. Let your heart live forever!" (Ps. 22:24, 26). The afflicted one must develop a lifestyle of seeking the Lord to remain in that place of satisfaction. David did not dichotomize soul and body. The inner and outer man were inseparably linked and godly help addressed both. Like Moses, he was faithful and dedicated (1 Sam. 22:14).

David loved God's words. The testimony of God concerning David's heart for His word came in one of God's conversations with David's son, Solomon. "And if you walk in My ways, keeping My statutes and commandments, as your father David walked, then I will prolong your days" (1 Kgs. 3:14). David kept the word of the Lord, His statutes and commandments. And this accolade was made with full knowledge of David's failures! David writes,

The law of the LORD is perfect, restoring the soul; The testimony of the LORD is sure, making wise the simple. The precepts of the LORD are right, rejoicing the heart; The commandment of the LORD is pure, enlightening the eyes. The fear of the LORD is clean, enduring forever; The judgments of the LORD are true; they are righteous altogether. They are more desirable than gold, yes, than much fine gold; Sweeter also than honey and the drippings of the honeycomb. Moreover, by them Your servant is warned; In keeping them there is great reward. (Ps. 19:7-11)

David asked God to search his heart (Ps. 139:23-24). The measuring stick, of course, was God's word. David wanted God's testimony. "You have tried my heart; You have visited me by night; You have tested me and You find nothing; I have purposed that my mouth will not transgress. As for the deeds of men, by the word of Your lips I have kept from the paths of the violent" (Ps. 17:3-4). It was not David's purpose to fall into sin and fail. He recognized that *by the words of Your lips*, he would live.

David's last words are provided in 2 Samuel 23. To David, God "Is as the light of the morning *when* the sun rises, A morning without clouds, When the tender grass *springs* out of the earth, Through sunshine after rain" (2 Sam. 23:4). David described himself as the anointed sweet psalmist of Israel. Although the House of the Lord was not mentioned directly, it seems obvious that much of his psalms were rooted in his experience of God's House. If he wasn't on the run to save his life, he was in and out of God's House. To remove the psalms of David from the context of God's House reduces their potency and benefit. A key to any lock is carefully filed, designed to open one lock, making the action of the key as simple and easy as possible. David had such a key to God's heart.

David described God as a clear, rising sun, yet in a way that allowed tender new grass shoots to receive the necessary rains and be able to grow. The springtime growth is a bridal experience (Song of Sol. 2:10-13). In contrast, he had only disdain for the disobedient. "But the worthless, every one of them will be thrust away like thorns, Because they cannot be taken in hand; But the man who touches them Must be armed with iron and the shaft of a spear, And they will be completely burned with fire in *their* place" (2 Sam. 23:6-7). In the end, the worthless can't be taken in hand. They are hardened. Tenderness and intimacy won't work. They must be held at a distance and eventually destroyed. God's polarizing effect was clearly seen by David. You either fall in love or you become untouchable. There is no middle ground.

Intimacy was the greatest aspect of David's life, singing and playing to the Lord, declaring God's words and calling on His name. He would dwell with the Lord whenever he could. He received correction and was broken-hearted over sin. He gave himself fully to pursuing the Lord—talent, time, and treasure. It is tempting to ask if David's heart overflowed and drove his experience in the House of the Lord or if it was the other way around? The answer is probably yes—to both. David was unlike Saul in almost every way. He was a man after God's own heart. The term *sharath* as used in relation to the Lord and His service changed dramatically under David. If intimacy alone was the sole benefit of God's House, it would have been sufficient for David, but he had an amazing revelation of God's House that would soon affect Israel and eventually, the rest of the world.

Chapter Nine

THE MODEL

D avid, like Moses, was given a divine revelation: "All
this, *said David*, the LORD made me understand in
writing by His hand upon me, all the details of this pattern"
(1 Chron. 28:19). He was given building dimensions, mate-
rials and the order of service. It is not clear when this revelation came to David, but the change in Israel's approach to
worship was dramatic.

David pitched a simple tent in Jerusalem, and in contrast to Saul, went to retrieve the Ark of the Covenant from
Abinadab's house. According to the pattern he had received,
he placed the Ark in this tent. It became the House of the
Lord or the House of God for a season. David appointed
288 Levitical prophetic singers and 4,000 band members
to *sharath* the Lord. It would be a night and day practice (1
Chron. 9:33), corporate, open to all. David gave the Levites
1 Chronicles 16 as their guide:

> He appointed some of the Levites as min-
> isters [sharath] before the ark of the LORD,
> ... Asaph the chief, ... with musical instru-
> ments, harps, lyres; also Asaph *played*

loud-sounding cymbals, … Then on that day David first assigned Asaph and his relatives to give thanks to the LORD. Oh give thanks to the LORD, call upon His name; Make known His deeds among the peoples. Sing to Him, sing praises to Him; Speak of all His wonders. Glory in His holy name; Let the heart of those who seek the LORD be glad. Seek the LORD and His strength; Seek His face continually. Remember His wonderful deeds which He has done, His marvels and the judgments from His mouth, O seed of Israel His servant, Sons of Jacob, His chosen ones! He is the LORD our God; His judgments are in all the earth. Remember His covenant forever, The word which He commanded to a thousand generations, The *covenant* which He made with Abraham, And His oath to Isaac. He also confirmed it to Jacob for a statute, To Israel as an everlasting covenant, Saying, To you I will give the land of Canaan, As the portion of your inheritance … Sing to the LORD, all the earth; Proclaim good tidings of His salvation from day to day. Tell of His glory among the nations, His wonderful deeds among all the peoples. For great is the LORD, and greatly to be praised; He also is to be feared above all gods … Splendor and majesty are before Him, Strength and joy are in His place. Ascribe to the LORD,

O families of the peoples, Ascribe to the
LORD glory and strength. Ascribe to the
LORD the glory due His name; Bring an
offering, and come before Him; Worship
the LORD in holy array. Tremble before
Him, all the earth; Indeed, the world is
firmly established, it will not be moved.
Let the heavens be glad, and let the earth
rejoice; And let them say among the nations,
"The LORD reigns." (1 Chron. 16:4-18,
23-26; 27-31)

In an instrumentally assisted and probably antiphonal
environment, they were commanded to sing, pray, give
thanks, praise, declare (ascribe), and agree with God's testimony—His covenant, commandments, judgments, and statutes; and call on His name. God's testimony became their
testimony, rehearsed before Him and each other. They did
this directly before the Ark of the Covenant in David's tent
where God's presence rested, certainly a stunning change of
events and departure from Moses! The ark that had been of
no interest to Saul or Israel was now center stage and fully
accessible to all. It did not go back to Gibeon where the tent
of meeting was located. It stood on its own. *Sharath*ing—
generating the remarkable, delightful and deeply satisfying experience *of* the Master had indeed changed. The
pattern God gave David was not the same as the one God
gave to Moses!

Davidic worship (instrumentally assisted worship and
intercession before the face of the Ark) went on continuously
(1 Chron. 16:37). Like Joshua, David was called to engage

with God's testimony night and day. There was a night watch (Ps. 134:1). David himself would at times awaken the dawn (Ps. 57:8-9). And he would come out morning, noon, and evening (Ps. 55:17) as his schedule permitted. The Levitical assignments were chosen by lot (1 Chron. 25:8), and their numbers supported a night and day schedule. They were trained in singing and as skillful musicians (1 Chron. 25:7). In the beginning, their fellow Levites provided for them (1 Chron. 9:33), so they would be free to do this full time.

It was loud and probably upbeat, definitely celebratory. David made *Davidic-worship*—night and day intercessory worship—a commanded practice (2 Chron. 35:15). The throngs of Israelites came as they had opportunity (Ps. 55:14) and presumably stood to pray and sing. They participated in the *sharath* of the Lord.

Worship, praise, thanksgiving, prayer, petition, supplication, song, rejoicing, and other similar nouns and verbs often overlap each other in meaning. It is like a friendly competition and is often challenging to tease out the distinctions because the terms all seem to be holding hands as they focus on the Lord. Mike Bickle has a helpful way to look at it: God wants our agreement—both personally as well as corporately—as David expressed it. When we agree verbally with who God is—His character and nature—either alone or in groups, we call it worship. When we agree with God's plans—His purposes in history—we call it intercession (Bickle, Contending for the Power of God 2003). Agreement can be spoken or sung.

The tent was a place of corporate testimony. It was a place to agree with God's very nature and worship Him. He was good (Ps. 31:19). He was holy (1 Chron. 16:10). He was altogether lovely (Ps. 27:4). It was a place to agree with God's plans and desires. He was going to rule the nations (Ps. 2). He was going to draw them (Ps. 22:27) to encounter Him. He was going to bring forth righteousness (Ps. 24:5). He was going to bless the land (Deut. 31:20) and Jerusalem (Ps. 51:18). Those in David's tent came into His presence and agreed with Him concerning His testimonies and ways and expressed it in instrumentally assisted song, worship, and intercession, day and night. This was the *sharath*—the sacrificial service *to* the Master from a forgiven, humble and intimate heart, generating the remarkable and deeply satisfying experience *of* the Master. *Sharath* was both an action taken and an experience received. David's tent was the House of the Lord (2 Sam. 12:20), and the Lord of the House was present.

It is not known if David followed Moses' practice of keeping a copy of the book of the law beside the Ark. It would have been a terrific spot for it. David loved to meditate in the presence of the Lord. With a little imagination, it would not be hard to see David or one of the Levitical singers run over to the table to search through the scroll that Moses had written and then back into worship, based on what God showed him. Proclaiming, singing, and praying the word was central to *sharath*ing the Lord. David's tent was a place where truth was showcased.

When David gave the Levites the charge to *sharath* the Lord, he commanded them to sing, pray, and declare the statutes and judgments and covenant of God (1 Chron. 16:14-17). They declared God's word before Him, the angels, demons, and all who came to the tent. They had a growing testimony. Moses had commanded the people: "You shall teach them diligently to your sons and shall talk of them when you sit in your house and when you walk by the way and when you lie down and when you rise up" (Deut. 6:7). David's tent was one more place to hear God's words rehearsed.

David gained an important insight in the arena of *sharath*ing. "And now my head will be lifted up above my enemies around me; And I will offer in His tent sacrifices of shouts of joy; I will sing, yes, I will sing praises to the LORD" (Ps. 27:6). This event took place *in* the tent. Proximity language was used. He was there. David offered a sacrifice *of shouts* (literally) of joy. No animal or grain sacrifice seemed to be in view. The shift away from burnt offerings to *living sacrifices* (Rom. 12:1) was in David's heart in some measure. The prophets picked up on this priority shift. Sacrificial heart first, burnt offering second. David went further and stated, "May my prayer be counted as incense before Thee; The lifting up of my hands as the evening offering" (Ps. 141:2). The burning of incense was linked to prayer as burnt offerings were linked to worship. The natural gave way to the spiritual. Incense and sacrifice with all their rich background and history could be replaced by their spiritual counterparts. The apostle John would later see this in operation in his heavenly revelation. Prayer was incense.

"Surely goodness and lovingkindness will follow me all the days of my life, And I will dwell in the House of the Lord forever" (Ps. 23:6). David was anointed and received revelation regarding the operation of the House of the Lord. But how much God revealed to him is not clear. David expected to do worship forever. He expected it to be sustainable. It was not a hundred-yard dash but a marathon. It was not the runner-up to revival, although revival occurred in conjunction with God's House. It was a destination. To see this as poetry expressing the quality of experience would be a small part of what David was communicating. David understood that the operation of God's House was a forever activity, even if his participation was interrupted by death for a season. He expected to pick it up again after death.

David noted that *sharath*ing was not simply a role of the saints on earth. "The LORD has established His throne in the heavens, And His sovereignty rules over all. Bless the LORD, you His angels, Mighty in strength, who perform His word, Obeying the voice of His word! Bless the LORD, all you His hosts, You who serve Him, doing His will" (Ps. 103:19-21). This is how heaven operates. The host of heaven *sharath*ed the Lord, too! The service or *sharath* of the Lord was not tactical and short term. It was strategic and eternal. The apostle John would later add to this revelation.

No regular sacrifice or Mosaic service and management activities appeared to be part of the *sharath*ing in David's tent. The Ark was present, but the other artifacts of Moses' tent of meeting apparently were not. Before taking a deeper look at David, we take pause to consider two potential concerns regarding the correctness of the night and day prayer model: (1) David's apparent deviation from Moses' pattern for the tabernacle; and (2) What pure source material can be used for David and his perspectives as opposed to the opinion of a later editor? Although neither issue can be addressed to the satisfaction of all, reasonable conclusions can be drawn from the text.

> Then Solomon, and all the assembly with
> him, went to the high place which was at

> Gibeon; for God's tent of meeting was there, which Moses the servant of the LORD had made in the wilderness. However, David had brought up the ark of God from Kiriath-jearim to the place he had prepared for it; for he had pitched a tent for it in Jerusalem. Now the bronze altar, which Bezalel the son of Uri, the son of Hur, had made, was there before the tabernacle of the LORD, and Solomon and the assembly sought it out. (2 Chron. 1:3-5)

David brought the Ark to Jerusalem amidst great celebration (2 Sam. 6:17) and provided burnt offerings and peace offerings to the Lord. He gave the Levites their assignment to *sharath* the Lord, blessed the people in the name of the Lord, and sent them home. Asaph was left in charge of David's tent, and Zadok the priest oversaw the sacrifices in Moses' tent at Gibeon. According to the instructions of 1 Chronicles 16, the Levitical singers and musicians had assignments at both Gibeon and Jerusalem. They brought to Gibeon their new aspects of *sharath*ing (1 Chron. 6:32).

The service in Jerusalem was night and day, while the service in Gibeon was around the morning (9:00 a.m.) and evening (3 p.m.) sacrifices. Presumably on feast or festival days and weeks, the normal daily service was extended. This arrangement of separate but shared resources continued until the eleventh year of Solomon, when the temple was completed and both services, Mosaic and Davidic, were housed in the same location.

> Then Solomon offered burnt offerings to
> the LORD on the altar of the LORD which
> he had built before the porch; and *did so*
> according to the daily rule, offering *them*
> up according to the commandment of
> Moses, for the Sabbaths, the new moons
> and the three annual feasts—the Feast of
> Unleavened Bread, the Feast of Weeks and
> the Feast of Booths. Now according to the
> ordinance of his father David, he appointed
> the divisions of the priests for their service,
> and the Levites for their duties of praise and
> ministering before the priests according to
> the daily rule, and the gatekeepers by their
> divisions at every gate; for David the man of
> God had so commanded. (2 Chron. 8:12-14)

The Chronicler made it clear that two independent streams or elements of worship were brought together by Solomon: David's focus on ministering (*sharath*ing) through night and day praise and intercession, and Moses' focus on sacrifice and the *sharath* associated with it. Prior to Solomon, no attempt was made to merge the two heavenly patterns into one. Night and day Davidic worship in Jerusalem functioned on its own for approximately forty-three years.

Interestingly, God put His name in Jerusalem, and the first occupant was David's tent. It was only later that sacrifice was transferred from the high place of Gibeon to Jerusalem. The older (Moses) would serve the younger (David). It would be through David that Jesus and the kingdom would come; and because of Jesus, burnt offerings and their supporting activities would eventually end. What David did was clear to the Chronicler. Why he did it and how he did it takes more investigation.

That two holy sites existed during David's time is clear. Some would argue that David's tent in Jerusalem followed Moses' pattern for the tabernacle. There would have been two tents connected: the Holy of Holies containing the Ark connected to and veiled from the Holy Place, containing incense altar, table for the show bread, and candelabra, and outside, the laver and altar for burnt offerings managed by the priests. This would make all the artifacts available to David in Jerusalem but would make the need for Gibeon questionable. If King David knew that the divinely declared location for God's habitation was Jerusalem (Ps. 132:13) and that Moses' tent was the approved sacrificial system, then his actions to create his own tent while supporting both locations were very strange. Why not bring everything to Jerusalem?

Although David's tent doesn't appear to have been a duplicate of Moses' tent, it does seem that some Mosaic activity did go on in Jerusalem prior to Solomon.

David wrote, "I shall wash my hands in innocence, And I will go about Thine altar, O LORD, That I may proclaim with the voice of thanksgiving, And declare all Thy wonders. O LORD, I love the habitation of Thy house, And the place where Thy glory dwells" (Ps. 26:6-8). It isn't clear in this context which altar was in view. The bronze altar of the tent of meeting was in Gibeon. The Chronicler spoke about the holy utensils in Gibeon rather than itemizing them (2 Chron. 5:5). Only the bronze altar was specifically mentioned as being in Gibeon. It is reasonable to assume the Mosaic altar of incense and laver were in Gibeon, too. David did share worship leaders between Jerusalem and Gibeon. He used the term *habitation* in Psalm 26:8, which would seem odd in Gibeon without the Ark. It is unlikely David traveled to Gibeon to wash his hands and then return to Jerusalem to the place where the glory dwelled. There might have been a laver or incense altar in Jerusalem. How they would operate in Jerusalem, if they were being regularly used, is not spelled out. It is possible that the Ark, which was portable, commuted between Jerusalem and Gibeon according to some schedule, perhaps for high feast days. But there is no mention of this in the scripture. As the Chronicler noted, praise and ministering before the Lord were the focus of David's tent. Regular sacrifice went on in Gibeon. This should be our understanding, too.

The account in 1 Chronicles 16 indicates David offered sacrifices. The altar in the dedication of 1 Chronicles 16 was likely one David had built for that purpose and could be reused as needed. There was no information on how David arranged his tent for the Lord. The Ark was all that was specifically mentioned. Since it was a night and day practice, it is reasonable to assume that lighting was available for the night watch. But how this would be done is not identified. And Solomon moved nothing to the temple outside of the Ark (2 Chron. 8:11–14; 1 Kgs. 8:1). All the temple artifacts were new. The bronze altar at Gibeon and other Moses-era artifacts most likely were retired and stored to avoid inappropriate veneration or competition with Jerusalem.

Some have suggested David's departure from Moses was sin and God passed over this (Rom. 3:25). This would explain two distinct centers of worship but would cast aspersions on what went on in Jerusalem. If it was truly sin, even though not willful or flagrant, would God remain silent? This seems unlikely, given examples of God's judgment upon later sinful acts of David. God had clear biblical expectations, which He enforced.

God did not pass over David's sin in transporting the Ark of the Covenant on a cart or his sin with Uriah and Bathsheba. Additionally, when David conducted an unapproved census of the people, he was again convicted, repented, and sacrificed on Araunah's threshing floor—the future site of Solomon's temple—to stop God's judgment plague from advancing further. He had a tender heart toward God. To keep the Ark from being housed in Moses' tent as prescribed would surely have been a significant error worthy of rebuke or correction. It would not be passed over. No rebuke ever came.

The Chronicler wrote, "Then David the king went in and sat before the LORD and said, Who am I, O LORD God, and what is my house that You have brought me this far?" (1 Chron. 17:16). Sitting before the Lord was literal—he sat before the Ark (lit. sitting before the face). If David had followed Moses' model when he set up his tent, this exceptional access to God might have been acceptable for him as it was for Moses, but certainly for no one else. Yet this general restriction was lifted for David's tent. In Moses' tent, the Levites were not even allowed to see the Ark, much less stand before it singing and playing night and day.

It is appropriate, therefore, to conclude that David set up his tent in Jerusalem with only the Ark and made no attempt to follow Moses. He did this at God's direction. Some supporting equipment, laver, incense altar, and altar for burnt offerings were present, but played an unscripted and irregular role. The purpose of this tent was the night and day *sharath* of the Lord.

The question around David's apparent deviation from Moses' model is further complicated by our second concern: accurate source material. Psalms with David's name are assumed to be David's compositions rather than a later school of David. A school of David may well have existed after David's time and is perfectly legitimate. However, the determination of which Psalms are truly David's and period-specific as opposed to a later school of David, writing at a future time, is speculative and at best inferential unless there are clear historical markers.

This is significant because David operated the House of the Lord out of his tent in Jerusalem and not out of Solomon's temple or Moses' tent of meeting. A Davidic school that came after David's death would have operated in the temple that was set up differently than David's tent. When David spoke of the House of the Lord or used similar expressions, he was speaking of his tent in Jerusalem. When Solomon or later writers spoke of the House of the Lord, they were referring to Solomon's temple.

The Psalm titles are taken at face value. If no authorship is provided, then David is not assumed to be the author. Some Psalms of David are from the wilderness years prior to the time of David's tent. Undoubtedly, David's understanding of God's heart and His revelation developed from the time he was anointed as a young man and the Spirit rushed over him. The embryo of Davidic worship matured over time. The actual tent of David and Davidic worship emerged after he had already been king in Hebron for seven years.

If Psalm 26, for example, was written during the time of Solomon's temple and not by David himself, then difficulties around the laver and sacrifice previously discussed would disappear. Under Solomon, David's tent and Mosaic sacrifice had been brought together in one location in Jerusalem. Everything was in Jerusalem. Davidic authorship of Psalm 26 does not create insurmountable issues as previously discussed. It should be accepted as given rather than appeal to a later *School of David writer.*

Psalm 28 offers another look at the *later Davidic writer* problem. David wrote, "Hear the voice of my supplications when I cry to You for help, When I lift up my hands toward Your holy sanctuary" (Ps. 28:2). In this Psalm, the term *debir* (rear room, the cubical Holy of Holies) is used and translated *sanctuary*. The term, when the city of that name is not in view, is only used in reference to the temple construction. It is not used for Moses' tent. At first glance, this would be reason enough to assume that a *later Davidic writer* had written this Psalm. If this Psalm is part of a Davidic collection that came after the temple was built, rather than from David himself, then it would make good sense. The Psalmist was standing in the courtyard, lifting his hands towards the Holy of Holies and making his request as Solomon directed the people to do.

If David was the author, as assumed, and the later group of Davidic writers is not in view, then more analysis is required. C.F. Keil and F. Delitzcsh saw the word "as the hinder part of the tent, from Arabic *dabara*, to be behind, whence the Talmudic *dubr*—that which is behind" (Keil and Delitzcsh 1975, Introduction, 364). The Ark may have simply been in the back part of David's tent as opposed to the middle or front. It would follow then that David was standing in the tent and lifting his hands in prayer toward the Ark in the back of the tent. Most likely, it was still respectfully draped, but the musicians and others like David, would be able to draw near. No information on the size or openness of David's tent is provided. It may well have had removable flaps to allow for larger groups of worshipers. Since this is a reasonable explanation for the use of *debir*, and David is considered the author, it should be preferred.

David was advanced in age when Solomon was anointed king. Adonijah, David's son, sought to be king and pulled together an alliance and developed a plan to have himself named as David's successor. The plan came to light, and David was warned. David had to move swiftly to counteract Adonijah's careful plan. Zadok the priest was commanded to immediately anoint Solomon king. "Zadok the priest then took the horn of oil from the tent and anointed Solomon. Then they blew the trumpet, and all the people said, *Long* live King Solomon!" (1 Kgs. 1:39).

During the short notice coronation of Solomon, Zadok took the anointing oil from the tent. Since this occurred in Jerusalem, the tent was assumed to be David's tent that housed the Ark. The setup of David's tent was not provided in any of the accounts, but it would seem there was a table or storage place for the anointing oil. The setup may have been similar to Shiloh, where there were other structures in the compound in addition to the tent that contained the Ark.

Since Levitical resources were shared across David's and Moses' tents and Zadok was the high priest, he probably made the trip between the two centers on a regular basis and had anointing oil kept in Jerusalem either in David's tent or in another tent in the compound.

Why Moses' tent of meeting in Gibeon and David's tent in Jerusalem remained separated remains a mystery. Solomon started the temple in the fourth year of his reign and finished in the eleventh. David reigned from Jerusalem for thirty-three years. For approximately forty-four years, David's tent remained separate and apart, yet open to God's worshipers.

What David did seems to be clear, but why he did it, apart from the command of God, is not. It may well be that the distinction between David's tent and Moses' tent would have a future significance. The amazing and open access to God's presence in David's tent may well have been a taste of things to come. The lasting reality would come later (Heb. 9:11-12). We are often called to obey God when the reason or outcome is not clear to us at the time. David obeyed the Word of the Lord. David followed the command of God. His successor, Solomon, and future faithful kings followed the command of David.

Isaiah would later describe God's House as a House of Prayer. This phrase will be adopted here to refer specifically to Davidic worship as he defined it for the Levites and worshipers in God's House—David's tent—the night and day corporate offering that mixes instrumentally supported worship and intercession before the face of the Lord. It is agreement with God in declaration and song. Worship (declaring God's attributes) and intercession (declaring God's purposes in the earth) would flow from the Scriptures (God's testimony). The worshipers remind God what He has written and promised in His Word and they call forth its fulfillment.

This partnership with the Master is offered *from* a forgiven and intimate heart and generates the remarkable and deeply satisfying experience *of* the Master—the *sharath* of the Lord.

The heart to *sharath* is most clearly seen in David's life. His life-long passionate pursuit in and out of the tent fueled the ongoing sharath of the Lord. *Sharath*ing the Lord was clearly *job one* for David, but God had additional elements of the House of Prayer that He would reveal through David and his heirs.

Chapter Ten

HOUSE OF PRAYER MISSION

From David's writing, it seems clear that experiencing God was a direct benefit of time in the House of the Lord. The Bridegroom God wants to touch our hearts and He wants us to touch His. Intimacy and friendship are essential in any relationship. As noted, it is first priority. The Ephesian church was corrected for losing their first love. They were busy doing. The doing was not the issue. The loss of first love devotion was. David's House of Prayer addressed, encouraged, and promoted intimacy. The House of Prayer had an audience of one—the Lord. The great devotion came first! David was a First Commandment saint.

Busyness is not the only challenge to intimacy. Sin kills intimacy. David asked a critical question, "Who may ascend into the hill of the LORD? And who may stand in His holy place?" (Ps. 24:3) and then provided the answer: "He who has clean hands and a pure heart, who has not lifted up his soul to falsehood And has not sworn deceitfully" (Ps. 24:4). He declared that the lowly man with clean hands and heart could ascend the hill of the Lord to His house, David's tent. The challenge for David was, "How do I get and keep clean hands?" David would learn two key elements.

He made his first discovery over his sin with Bathsheba. Only God could wipe away transgression. Only God could clean hands. David cried out, "Be gracious to me, O God, according to Your lovingkindness; According to the greatness of Your compassion blot out my transgressions. Wash me thoroughly from my iniquity And cleanse me from my sin" (Ps. 51:1-2). It is the gracious and compassionate God who applies that forgiveness to our souls. It is God's gift. Yet, every gift must be opened and received; otherwise it only remains the kind intention of a giver.

David discovered that forgiveness was not mechanical. No earthly effort or offering will satisfy the offense before God. "For You do not delight in sacrifice, otherwise I would give it; You are not pleased with burnt offering. The sacrifices of God are a broken spirit; A broken and a contrite heart, O God, You will not despise" (Ps. 51:16-17). David would gladly have given a burnt offering to cover his sin with Bathsheba, but he knew it was not sufficient. Sin is costly. God was looking for a burnt heart, not just burnt sacrifices (Ps. 51:3-10).

David would confess his iniquity and receive God's gift of forgiveness. His sin was ultimately against God (Ps. 51:4). When David was confronted with sin, he didn't harden his heart. He confessed his sin, received forgiveness, and got back up and went hard for God. The Lord gave him clean hands, which was a prerequisite for ascending the hill of the Lord to abide in His tent (Ps. 15:1). This gift of clean hands and a restored heart was part of God's testimony. Though the earthly impact of sin was disastrous for David, the heavenly impact of his sin was impossible for David to bear. David could not tolerate being separated from his God. He wanted truth in his innermost being. He wanted to know joy and gladness. Sickness had attacked his bones, and he longed to have his iniquities hidden from God's face. He wanted a clean heart and a steadfast spirit.

David would cultivate faithfulness again (Ps. 51:12-15). He did not put himself on probation. He did not give himself a time-out for sin or pull back into a world of shame and disqualify himself from God's mercy. He recognized his tendency to go astray and asked God to scrutinize him (Ps. 139:23-24). David's large failing with Bathsheba was not the only failing in David's life. He had other sins and must have humbly discovered that having clean hands and heart was not a *one and done* event. It takes humility to ascend God's hill, and it takes humility to stay. Only God would and could clean hands—repeatedly. Only the humble would ask Him to do this. It is the perfect preparation for the bride and a requirement of the House of Prayer.

The condition of David's heart was a big deal to him. After many years of having the House of Prayer, David must have been aware of those who showed up to *sharath* out of habit rather than heart. The external visible practice doesn't guarantee the internal condition of the heart. The prophets would have a great deal to say about practice and heart in later years. Practice may be able to jumpstart the heart, but it can't sustain it. Exposing his heart to God was the best way to maintain integrity of practice and heart. David's intercessory worship would come from a forgiven heart and clean hands.

Yet there was more. David had a second great revelation about the forgiven man. "He shall receive a blessing from the LORD And righteousness from the God of his salvation.

This is the generation of those who seek Him, Who seek Your face—*even* Jacob. Selah" (Ps. 24:5-6). The blessing of the Lord, even the righteousness from His hand and forgiveness that was applied to our souls, belonged to the generation that would seek Him. The forgiven man would be the seeking man. He would open the gift. Receive. The embarrassment over sin—even repeated failure—would not restrain the seeker. There must be a desire to ascend the hill of the Lord; to overcome all the difficulties that keep us from God's face, and to cultivate a heart (Ps. 27:8) that stays in His presence forever (Ps. 23:6). The Bridegroom God wanted a restored relationship, not simply absolution. God would handle his transgression and clean his hands and heart whenever he came to Him. He was looking for a bride. Intimacy without clean hands and a seeking heart is impossible.

David certainly had days when he slipped in and out of the tent because of his many responsibilities, but he wanted more. He did not want to be socially religious. He wanted to abide there. David asked, "Who may abide in Thy tent? Who may dwell on Thy holy hill?" (Ps. 15:1) It must have been an odd question to David's listeners. With the busyness of life, no one could abide. Why desire something you can't have? It must be hyperbole, a figure of speech. There were simply too many things to do. Dwelling and intimacy were optional in David's day, as they are in our day. Abiding, both the desire for it and the struggle to practice it, is the domain of lovers, the bride and Bridegroom.

David would take God's requirement for dwelling and apply it to his own house and kingdom. "My eyes shall be upon the faithful of the land that they may dwell with me; He who walks in a blameless way is the one who will minister to me. He who practices deceit shall not dwell within my house; He who speaks falsehood shall not maintain his position before me" (Ps. 101:6-7). The blameless—those whose hands were clean—would *sharath* the Lord and David. "As for the saints who are in the earth, they are the majestic ones in whom is all my delight" (Ps. 16:3). Apparently, the *sharath* of the Lord makes it difficult to apply any other standard to or have any other expectation for the saints around you.

It was up to the faithful to seek Him and set their hearts and repeatedly reset them to be in His presence. Those who practice deceit might drop into the tent from time to time but wouldn't and couldn't stay long. As in David's court, they would not retain their position. The House of Prayer was a filter and thermometer! It had a built-in exit strategy for the deceitful. It refined. The dross came to the top for removal. The only way to retain the dross was to leave or not come to the House of Prayer at all. David declared, "For You are not a God who takes pleasure in wickedness; No evil dwells with You. The boastful shall not stand before Your eyes; You hate all who do iniquity" (Ps. 5:4-5).

Those who make no time for the House of Prayer might want to check their hands to see if uncleanness has crept in or if the desire to seek the Lord has waned and the heart has hardened. The door is open for those who wish to come and those who wish to leave.

Like Moses' tent of meeting, God's bridegroom heart was available to the lover but protected from the deceitful and wayward. The House of Prayer helped filter out those without a First Commandment zeal. It filtered out those with little or no inclination, desire or perseverance. The

Bridegroom God had chosen to be found by those who earnestly sought Him—though on the surface, waiting and adversity seemed to be at odds with a bridegroom heart. Love will stand the test of time. It is dedicated and will have nothing else. Joseph, Moses, Aaron, Joshua, Samuel, and David did indeed draw near to the Lord in spite of their circumstances. The impact of their choices made history.

Intimacy, dwelling, and maintaining clean hands were top priorities for David, but he revealed much more about the nature and mission of the House of Prayer.

Psalm 57 was penned by David when he was on the run from Saul. His circumstances were dire. In a moment of reflection, he set his heart: he would awaken the dawn. With harp and lyre he would sing. He knew he would sing before the people—and more significantly before the nations— which was an impossibility at that moment. Later as king when the House of Prayer was running, and looking to defeat Edom, David would pray the same way. "Awake, harp and lyre; I will awaken the dawn! I will give thanks to Thee, O LORD, among the peoples; And I will sing praises to Thee among the nations" (Ps. 108:2-3).

A fully functioning House of Prayer would draw the nations. David may have used poetic repetition to show the intensity of his commitment, as some suggest. However, David believed he would actually sing before foreigners. Amazing! David wrote:

> O You who hear prayer, To You all men come. Iniquities prevail against me; As for our transgressions, You forgive them. How blessed is the one whom You choose and

bring near to *You* To dwell in Your courts. We will be satisfied with the goodness of Your house, Your holy temple. By awesome *deeds* You answer us in righteousness, O God of our salvation, You who are the trust of all the ends of the earth and of the farthest sea. (Ps. 65:2-5)

God answers prayer, and all people are hard-wired for prayer, without exception. Literally, all flesh would come to God's courts, David's tent. They are wired to come to God. Men resist this urge naturally because of their personal iniquities. God forgives iniquity and opens the door to dwelling. He draws men from the nations to dwell in His courts where they are deeply satisfied. In fact, God Himself would draw them. David instructs those already dwelling in His courts to call out for awesome deeds, literally fearful (Hebrew *yare*) or marvelous (LXX *thaumastos*) deeds that God answers. The nations will trust in Him.

With a little imagination, it is not hard to see the saints of David's tent leaving for a time, roving the marketplace and nearby villages, praying awesome deeds over anyone who would receive their ministry, or simply inviting them to the House of Prayer where they encountered the living God and experienced His awesome deeds. The House of Prayer was a mission strategy. Its intense vertical focus would overflow to the nations. David's team would declare God's testimony (which had become their testimony) before the foreigners God would draw.

David's son, Solomon, prayed that God would answer the prayers of the foreigners who were drawn to the temple because of the fame of God's name (2 Chron. 6:32-33). He asked God to watch over the courts day and night (2 Chron. 6:20-22), to respond to the prayers offered either directly from the courts or offered toward the courts from a great distance.

The Queen of Sheba may have been one of the most famous visitors to Jerusalem. She had heard of the fame of the name as reported by Solomon (1 Kgs. 10:1). She was a wealthy woman and brought a sizeable gift to Solomon.

> When the queen of Sheba perceived all the wisdom of Solomon, the house that he had built, the food of his table, the seating of his servants, the attendance of his waiters and their attire, his cupbearers, and his stairway by which he went up to the House of the Lord, there was no more spirit in her. (1 Kgs. 10:4-5)

No doubt Solomon's buildings were marvelous; but for a woman of great means, buildings, food, and servants, their attire and service—all reflecting great prosperity—were not unknown to her. Yet, what she saw left her breathless. It is hard to imagine that a stairway would have this impact on her. Not much is known about such a stairway. Ahaz removed a covered way from his house to the temple because of the king of Assyria (2 Kgs. 16:18). No mention of it is made in Solomon's plans. What would take her breath away?

She saw Solomon's *ascent* that the translator interpreted as stairway. This term appeared at the end of the list that amazed the queen. Is it possible that what she saw was the *ascent* to the House of Prayer and not a staircase? There are fifteen Psalms of *ascent*—same Hebrew word group as stairway. David described the procession—the ascent, into God's presence. "They have seen Thy procession, O God, The procession of my God, my King, into the sanctuary. The singers went on, the musicians after them, In the midst of the maidens beating tambourines" (Ps. 68:24-25). It isn't known if this Psalm reflected a one-time inaugural event when David put up his tent, or whether it was related to the turnover of musicians and singers coming in to relieve the current set of Levites. This may well have been what the Queen of Sheba later saw when she visited Solomon and saw the temple in operation. She may have awakened at night and heard the sound of celebration in the courts, or stopped by at the morning or evening sacrifice, and saw it was still going strong. She stopped by again the next day and the next and the next week. She realized this went on 24/7. If she asked Solomon for an explanation and discovered the Levites were singing, declaring, and interceding according to the statutes, judgments, and testimony of God, and the people of God came out when they could to pray, that may have left her breathless. No one in the world did that!

The queen asked Solomon tough questions. "And Solomon answered all her questions; nothing was hidden from the king which he did not explain to her" (1 Kgs. 10:3). The text does not specifically identify the questions asked, but it is not hard to imagine that the queen may have questioned Solomon closely about the testimonies, statutes, and judgments she heard.

The House of Prayer was not only an evangelism strategy. It was also a defense for the city, as Solomon's imagery suggests. Solomon's reflections on the temple he had built are important. "Unless the LORD builds the house, They labor in vain who build it; Unless the LORD guards the city, The watchman keeps awake in vain" (Ps. 127:1). If God was not behind the House of Prayer and wasn't guarding the city, then the natural and intercessory watchman would add little value to the security of the city. But the Lord does build the house and provide the watchman on the wall. God guards the city. Solomon connected the House of Prayer to guarding the city. God's House operated night and day. His watchman would speak up in His courts, and He would back up the security of the city.

> To which the tribes go up, even the tribes of the LORD—An ordinance for Israel—To give thanks to the name of the LORD. For there thrones were set for judgment, The thrones of the house of David. Pray for the peace of Jerusalem: May they prosper who love you. May peace be within your walls, And prosperity within your palaces. For the sake of my brothers and my friends, I will now say, May peace be within you. For the sake of the House of the Lord our God, I will seek your good. (Ps. 122:4-9)

The House of Prayer was God's strategic citywide solution, not only for security as Solomon declared, but for prosperity as well. David commanded that prayer for the peace and prosperity of Jerusalem should be offered. It was a House of Prayer responsibility and opportunity. Additionally, David understood something of the significance of Jerusalem. The writer of Psalm 132 provided further insight: "For the LORD has chosen Zion; He has desired it for His habitation. This is My resting place forever; Here I will dwell, for I have desired it" (Ps. 132:13-14). David cares about God's desires. God loves the city of Jerusalem. John the apostle described Jerusalem as a bride. God would discipline the city and its Jewish occupants but would never abandon it. The throne of the house of David would be there. This was an unconditional promise of God. He would make it happen.

David was aware of the evil operating in his city as well. "Confuse, O Lord, divide their tongues, For I have seen violence and strife in the city. Day and night they go around her upon her walls; And iniquity and mischief are in her midst. Destruction is in her midst; Oppression and deceit do not depart from her streets" (Ps. 55:9-11). It is interesting to recognize that evil operates like intercession—day and night on the wall. It is organized and has vision over the city just like intercessors who are spiritual watchmen!

David would contend for the city.

> As for me, I shall call upon God, And the LORD will save me. Evening and morning and at noon, I will complain and murmur, And He will hear my voice. He will redeem my soul in peace from the battle which is against me, For they are many who strive with me. God will hear and answer them— Even the one who sits enthroned from of old—Selah. (Ps. 55:16-19)

At all times of the day, David would murmur, literally roar before the Lord. Evening has the normal sense of sundown but can include into the night (Gen. 1:5). Like a skilled advocate or lawyer, he would forcefully present his case—roar, in the courts of His God. The Judge would hear his case and save (deliver) His righteous petitioner.

As it was with Moses in the wilderness, God's courts were open day and night. Evil had already made this connection and wanted to leverage its position over the city. David had his legal staff singing and declaring God's promises and statutes to the sound of the lyre night and day in God's courts. The House of Prayer blessed the city and cried out for its provision. The House of Prayer guarded the city, holding its gates (Ps. 24:7); welcoming friends, denying enemies entrance as appropriate, and attacking any evil that had slipped in through those gates. The battle for the city, whether from within or without, whether to bless or oppose, never stops and neither should Davidic intercessory worship.

Jerusalem is clearly the city in view for David and Solomon, but Malachi will later open the door to a broader understanding. There would be other locations.

David saw his tent as a place of refuge.

> Wondrously show Your lovingkindness, O Savior of those who take refuge at Your right hand From those who rise up *against* them. Keep me as the apple of the eye; Hide me in the shadow of Your wings From the wicked who despoil me, My deadly enemies who surround me. (Ps. 17:7-9)

Standing in the shadow of the wings of the cherubim quieted his heart even though he was well aware of his enemies. He was hidden. David saw the tent as a place of refuge—a hiding place. It was safe. The fabric of the material didn't make it safe, but the appeal to the one sitting on the mercy seat did. And evil didn't like the presence of the Lord. He wanted to be kept or guarded in his *apple of the eye* experience of God. The House of Prayer was a place to reinforce his focus and encourage his heart. The apple of His eye is bridal language.

> How great is Your goodness, Which You have stored up for those who fear You, Which You have wrought for those who take refuge in You, Before the sons of men! You hide them in the secret place of Your presence from the conspiracies of man; You keep them secretly in a shelter from the strife of tongues. (Ps. 31:19-20)

David had peace of mind in the secret place of God's tent. Conspiracies didn't disappear, but their impact on David was greatly diminished because of his time in God's presence. The refuge was in God—literally. David was not making a pilgrimage to a sacred place or touching sacred artifacts, He was in God's presence. He would write that it was a place without the experience of condemnation (Ps. 34:21-22). God was clearly good. For those who feared the Lord and dwelled in God's presence, the full measure of God's refuge was available.

At times David struggled emotionally, yet he discovered that he could battle back from depression in God's tent (Ps. 22). As he began writing Psalm 22, he felt utterly forsaken. His day was like his night. He found no relief. The actual event that triggered David's depression was not provided, but he was at an exceedingly low point in his life. He felt great reproach and his self-esteem almost crashed completely. The comments and sneers of others impacted him physically. He was ill. All his bones were out of joint. He cried to God for help and began to battle back. He would declare God's name in the assembly. He would pay his vows before those who feared the Lord. He reminded his heart that those who seek Him will praise Him. All the families of the nations would worship before Him. Praise and declarations overwhelmed his heart. It is not clear if his recovery started outside the tent, but his declaration to seek and praise the Lord among the assembly—those who feared the Lord and regularly gathered in the courts—and his call for the nations to come and worship suggest that David finished his recovery in the tent. His practice jumpstarted his heart. The tent was a healing place, a refuge.

> How precious is Your lovingkindness, O God! And the children of men take refuge in the shadow of Your wings. They drink their fill of the abundance of Your house; And You give them to drink of the river of Your delights. For with You is the fountain of life; In Your light we see light. (Ps. 36:7-9)

It was in the shadow of His wings that David discovered abundance. His heart came alive. The tent was a place to drink your fill. And God released His delight in the tent and that delight followed David in tangible ways when David went out to do life. Being rightly connected to the King of the universe was life. It was the source of life. Having a soul and spirit that are full makes the trials of life bearable. The world is not sure God exists; or if He does, He is aloof and far away—a clinical, unfeeling God. Not so for the one who dwells in His presence. The provision of God comes from the presence of God for those who have set their hearts to seek and know Him. He is looking for those who will stay, who want to dwell with Him. God wants to give much more.

The House of Prayer was also a place of insight. Because of God's light, David and those who feared the Lord would see light in His light or have revelation. They would have understanding and a measure of clarity that His light brings. The scriptures came alive, and as Moses had declared, God would give insight into difficult cases in the place that He had chosen.

Personal petitions had a home in the House of Prayer also. God not only cared about nations and cities, especially Jerusalem, but about the simple requests of saints.

> May He send you help from the sanctuary And support you from Zion! May He remember all your meal offerings And find your burnt offering acceptable! Selah. May He grant you your heart's desire And fulfill all your counsel! We will sing for joy over your victory, And in the name of our God

> we will set up our banners. May the LORD
> fulfill all your petitions. (Ps. 20:2-5)

David wanted God to fulfill all the petitions offered in the House of Prayer. Help comes from the sanctuary in Zion (David's tent). God cares about the heart's desire and wants to take counsel with petitioners. This is the Bridegroom God. Victory is literally salvation. There is a celebratory note in advance of the petition's fulfillment and a desire for the petitioner's testimony.

"O God, *You are* awesome from Your sanctuary. The God of Israel Himself gives strength and power to the people. Blessed be God!" (Ps. 68:35). David saw the tent of the Lord as a place of resource. God will provide—from His sanctuary.

The House of Prayer was also a place of fellowship. David provided a unique insight into fellowship as noted earlier. "We who had sweet fellowship together Walked in the house of God in the throng" (Ps. 55:14). Sweet fellowship is connected to walking together in the House of Prayer. David used the term that is translated *throng*. It has a basic meaning of an *undifferentiated group, in agreement*. It has the flavor of one bride. No doubt there were different camps in Israel— perhaps similar to the concept of Christian denominations. However, the place of prayer produced an undifferentiated heart. Other differences that often divide seem to diminish in the house. Fellowship or unity is often a natural byproduct of the House of Prayer rather than something elusive we actively pursue. It becomes ours in prayer together. Real unity grows out of time before the face of God. David had this experience.

Unfortunately, unity is not always the byproduct. In this passage, David refers to a former friend and companion who had wounded him. The House of Prayer is not a panacea for life. Failure in relationships can occur anywhere—even among those in the house. God was in the tent, and a fiery passion for God before His face would normally lead to a love for one another. Time in the tent may be a barometer of what things we will forgive others and the forgiveness we will receive in return. If unity is low, then the lack of time together in His presence in prayer may be low as well.

There will be some who turn to evil, as David discovered, and must be given to the Lord. The fastest path to reconciliation may be in the tent. Those who can be reconciled, should. Time in the tent will surely help. Our hearts are softened, and once reconciled, the tent will help us keep it that way. Dwelling in the tent makes a difference.

Luke provided God's summary on David and the mission. "For David, after he had served the purpose of God in his own generation, fell asleep, and was laid among his fathers and underwent decay" (Acts 13:36). David had fulfilled God's purposes. Incredible. There was great mercy for the one who pursued and did not give up in discouragement—fully forgiven and fully energized to move forward with God. No false humility—self-inflicted punishment or withdrawal from God and the saints, as the self-righteous might be tempted to do. No living in shame and condemnation. He was a House of Prayer guy; a warrior, and fascinated lover, fully spiritual and fully natural—with no contradiction between the two, just like Jesus.

The great devotion, the *sharath* of the Lord, the First Commandment was the primary mission of the House of

Prayer. Yet God released so much more through David's tent. It was a mission strategy—drawing the nations—a spiritual defense and provision for the city, a place of refuge—a hiding place, abundance, resource, and a river of delights, a place of revelation, illumination, fellowship, and personal petition.

It is hard to move on into the Kings and Chronicles from here once David is in your heart, but trouble was on the horizon along with redemption. God would lay down more of the House of Prayer story.

Chapter Eleven

CHRONICLES AND KINGS

S olomon completed the temple in the eleventh year of
his reign. He brought the Ark of the Covenant into his
temple. The utensils from the tent of meeting in Gibeon were
also brought up (2 Chron. 5:5-6). Only the Ark was original.
All the other artifacts from Moses' tent were newly minted.
Solomon summoned all the people for the great dedication
of the temple. The Levites lifted their voices in one accord,
accompanied by musical instruments. They declared God's
goodness, and the temple was so filled with a cloud of glory
that the priests could not minister.

> The LORD said to him, I have heard your
> prayer and your supplication, which you
> have made before Me; I have consecrated
> this house which you have built by putting
> My name there forever, and My eyes and
> My heart will be there perpetually. As for
> you, if you will walk before Me as your
> father David walked, in integrity of heart
> and uprightness, doing according to all
> that I have commanded you *and* will keep

> My statutes and My ordinances, then I will establish the throne of your kingdom over Israel forever, just as I promised to your father David, saying, 'You shall not lack a man on the throne of Israel.' (1 Kgs. 9:3-5)

God promised His heart and His eyes would be in the temple perpetually. It was Bridegroom language. God's heart was moved by what went on in the temple courts.

David became the gold standard for Solomon and all future kings (1 Kgs. 14:7-8). Unfortunately, Solomon was not like his father David. He started well loving the Lord, but he left the door of disobedience open. He sacrificed and offered incense on the high places and loved many foreign women (1 Kgs. 3:2-4). He was unfaithful. And Israel became unfaithful. People and king looked alike.

> Now King Solomon loved many foreign women along with the daughter of Pharaoh: Moabite, Ammonite, Edomite, Sidonian, and Hittite women, from the nations concerning which the LORD had said to the sons of Israel, You shall not associate with them, nor shall they associate with you, *for* they will surely turn your heart away after their gods... For when Solomon was old, his wives turned his heart away after other gods; and his heart was not wholly devoted to the LORD his God, as the heart of David his father *had been.* (1 Kgs. 11:1-4)

Solomon was unequally yoked and followed the practices of his wives. He went after Ashtoreth, the goddess of the Sidonians; Milcom, the detestable idol of the Ammonites; Chemosh, the detestable idol of Moab; and Molech, the detestable idol of the sons of Ammon. God had often warned about the dangers of being unequally yoked. Regardless of the object placed ahead of God in devotion, idolatry was its root cause. For Solomon, it was his foreign wives. However, the list of idolatrous objects in the world that supplant or replace God is endless. This would not happen to His Son. God would provide a faithful bride, "that He might present to Himself the church in all her glory, having no spot or wrinkle or any such thing; but that she would be holy and blameless" (Eph. 5:27).

David gave Solomon the bridal pathway.

> As for you, my son Solomon, know the God of your father, and serve Him with a whole heart and a willing mind; for the LORD searches all hearts, and understands every intent of the thoughts. If you seek Him, He will let you find Him; but if you forsake Him, He will reject you forever. (1 Chron. 28:9)

God looked ahead in time and saw what was coming—the sin of Israel and the sin of Judah. He placed a small and surmountable barrier before His heart. They needed to diligently seek Him with a whole heart (Heb. 11:6). Sadly, this requirement would filter out many!

God established the procedure for national repentance. Solomon stood before the people in the temple courts on that inaugural day with the gathered Levitical singers and band members. He gave one of the most-quoted passages in the Old Testament. When the people disobeyed and encountered various distressful and disastrous events, they could return to the House of Prayer reality and find help.

> Then the LORD appeared to Solomon at night and said to him, "I have heard your prayer, and have chosen this place for Myself as a house of sacrifice. If I shut up the heavens so that there is no rain, or if I command the locust to devour the land, or if I send pestilence among My people, and My people who are called by My name humble themselves and pray, and seek My face and turn from their wicked ways, then I will hear from heaven, will forgive their sin, and will heal their land. Now My eyes will be open and My ears attentive to the prayer *offered* in this place" (2 Chron. 7:12-15).

Verse 14 is often quoted as a stand-alone prayer. Yet it comes in the context of the House of Prayer promise. It is a call to return to a House of Prayer heart and practice. To have a time of national repentance without embracing a call to return to the House of Prayer lifestyle would have seemed ridiculous to David in his time. Israel was always in trouble for dumbing down the First Commandment. To offer God a national prayer of repentance on the one hand, while rejecting His purposes and plans for the House of Prayer on the other hand, would hardly fly. He was watching attentively for prayer and was ready when the nation repented and returned. Repentance without return is only a confession of being *caught in the act*, as King Saul had demonstrated. It has little lasting value. A return to any House of Prayer substitute—business as usual religious practice—will die out soon enough. God wanted His people to return to the House of Prayer—heart, mind, and soul returning to the place of His intimacy.

Rehoboam succeeded Solomon as king. He was forty-one years old when he became king, and his mother was Naamah, an Ammonite.

> Judah did evil in the sight of the LORD, and they provoked Him to jealousy more than all that their fathers had done, with the sins which they committed. For they also built for themselves high places and *sacred* pillars and Asherim on every high hill and beneath every luxuriant tree. There were also male cult prostitutes in the land. (1 Kgs. 14:22-24)

It was a dark time. David's heart and practice were largely gone from king and people. Unfaithfulness in body and spirit was the order of the day. True to the word given Samuel, the people looked like the king, and neither was faithful.

Rehoboam sustained temple life, but only what was needed: "Then it happened as often as the king entered the House of the Lord that the guards would carry them [*bronze* shields] and would bring them back into the guards' room" (1 Kgs. 14:28). The term *as often* has the sense of "only as required—sufficiency, necessary supply, enough" (1975, Brown Driver Briggs 191). This stands in contrast to David, who was zealous for the House of Prayer. David was over the top in worship of the Lord, not simply offering the bare minimum, as did Rehoboam. Later, we will see that the Laodicean church of Revelation 3:16—neither hot nor cold— is a clear example of the *just enough* Rehoboam.

If sin had run its full course and there were neither temple nor courts and the nation had been deported, God would still listen. Israel had been exiled to Babylon and Daniel, one of the exiles, was elevated to the king's service. His heart was committed to remaining faithful to the Lord. Daniel's window faced toward Jerusalem, and he prayed three times a day (Dan. 6:10). It was his common practice. On the day he understood Jeremiah's prophecy of judgment had been fulfilled, he went into prayer to confess his sins and the sins of his nation. It was a long-distance, *2 Chronicles 7:14* prayer, most likely prayed from his Jerusalem-facing window. Daniel knew God's testimony and continued to agree and declare it. Exile was not God's ideal circumstance. He wished His people would recognize His discipline long before they had to be expelled from the land.

Daniel recognized that Jeremiah's seventy years had run their course. He cried out, "So now, our God, listen to the prayer of Your servant and to his supplications, and for Your sake, O Lord, let Your face shine on Your desolate sanctuary" (Dan. 9:17). God did respond to Daniel's prayer. A remnant did return and began to rebuild God's House—the House of Prayer. A 2 Chronicles 7:14 prayer that does not include a return to the House of Prayer will not be sustained. (Isaiah will have more to say on this in the next chapter.)

Asaph, one of the House of Prayer leaders, would pen God's heart cry:

> Gather My godly ones to Me, Those who have made a covenant with Me by sacrifice … I do not reprove you for your sacrifices, And your burnt offerings are continually before Me … Offer to God a sacrifice of thanksgiving, And pay your vows to the Most High; … He who offers a sacrifice of thanksgiving honors Me; And to him who orders *his* way *aright* I shall show the salvation of God. (Ps. 50:5-23)

Gather them to Me. Returning had a context. When they came, it was only to sacrifice. But the issue wasn't burnt offerings; it was their lack of participation in Davidic worship—the sacrifice of thanksgiving before Him—in the House of Prayer. God's House was a house of sacrifice as Solomon had indicated. But ultimately, it was the sacrifice of thanksgiving that was God's greatest desire. God would take care of burnt offerings Himself in the course of time. Living sacrifices—the spiritual service of worship—would remain even after blood sacrifice had been satisfied (Rom. 12:1).

The first full example of 2 Chronicles 7:14 came in Jehoshaphat's day. Asa, Jehoshaphat's father, was angry with God and angry with His seer. He had a severe disease in his feet. He sought his physicians but did not seek the Lord for help. Apparently, he died a very unhappy man. Jehoshaphat chose instead to follow the example of his father David.

A great army came up against Jehoshaphat (2 Chron. 20:1-20). He was afraid and turned his attention to seek the Lord. He proclaimed a fast and gathered Judah to the Lord's house to pray. The prophet Jahaziel told them not to fear. They wouldn't even need to fight the battle because it was the Lord's.

> When he had consulted with the people, he appointed those who sang to the LORD and those who praised *Him* in holy attire, as they went out before the army and said, Give thanks to the LORD, for His lovingkindness is everlasting. When they began singing and praising, the LORD set ambushes against the sons of Ammon, Moab and Mount Seir, who had come against Judah; so they were routed. (2 Chron. 20:21-22)

The House of Prayer was assembled. Young and old alike stood in the court of God's House to pray and praise Him. The prominence of the Davidic worship team was graphically validated. The worship team went out in front of the army. Intercession and praise were the key weapon of the army, and it was up front leading the way. God then acted in concert when their praise and intercession ascended.

The magnitude of spoils associated with the victory of the saints' intercession and the interdiction of the Lord on their behalf was amazing. It took three days for the army to transport the spoils of war to Jerusalem. "And they came to

Jerusalem with harps, lyres, and trumpets to the House of the Lord. And the dread of God was on all the kingdoms of the lands when they heard that the LORD had fought against the enemies of Israel" (2 Chron. 20:28-29).

The House of Prayer was functioning in Jerusalem and the dread of the Lord fell on the kingdoms around Judah in much the same way as the Ark produced deadly confusion among the Philistines when it was captured (1 Sam. 5:11). Perhaps the Philistine experience lived on in local folklore and found its way to the surrounding nations. Jehoshaphat's response to crisis was the model for national repentance prescribed by Solomon: crisis, return to the House of Prayer (repentance with humility), corporate worship and intercession, deliverance, and provision (spoils). David prayed for Jerusalem, but Jehoshaphat discovered the regional implications of the House of Prayer. The dread of God was operating.

Sadly, Jehoshaphat—like Solomon—did not keep his focus. He allied himself with the idolatrous King Ahaziah of Israel, who was the son of Ahab and Jezebel. Ahaziah's mother Jezebel was from Phoenicia and suppressed the prophets of God in Israel while strongly promoting Baal and Ashtoreth worship. Ahaziah walked in all the sins of his father Ahab. Jehoshaphat's commercial venture with Ahaziah was destroyed by God; there is no prosperity in disobedience.

More significantly, Jehoshaphat's son Jehoram married Jezebel's daughter, Athaliah (2 Chron. 21:6), and when he became king, he killed all his brothers. The story of being unequally yoked tragically lasted well beyond Jehoram's day.

Jehoram was a miserable king. His sons were killed by Arab raiders, and only Ahaziah remained (2 Chron. 22:1).

Athaliah, a granddaughter of Omri, king of Israel, was his mother. When her son Ahaziah became king, she coached him to do evil in the eyes of the Lord (2 Chron. 22:3). He reigned as king for only one year and died. Athaliah rose up and killed all the royal offspring except Joash, who had been hidden away in the House of the Lord by Jehoshabeath, the daughter of King Jehoram and wife of Jehoiada the priest. Athaliah ruled for six years until Jehoiada brought Joash out and made him king. It was time to celebrate.

> And all the people of the land rejoiced and blew trumpets, the singers with *their* musical instruments leading the praise. Then Athaliah tore her clothes and said, Treason! Treason! ... Moreover, Jehoiada placed the offices of the House of the Lord under the authority of the Levitical priests, whom David had assigned over the House of the Lord, to offer the burnt offerings of the LORD, as it is written in the Law of Moses—with rejoicing and singing according to the order of David. (2 Chron. 23:13, 18)

During the Joash revival, the Levitical singers and House of Prayer practice were restored in some measure. The focus was on the coronation events that required singers. It is not clear if Jehoiada provided Davidic support for sacrifice alone or the full House of Prayer. However, since it was at the command of David, and the desire to return to the Lord was present, it is probably fair to assume that the House of

Prayer was in the picture as well. The Chronicler referred to both Moses and David. Time had not blurred the distinctions between the two. Moses was the father of the sacrificial system and David the father of worship. Joash served the Lord all the days of Jehoiada the priest. After his death, the king and the people of the land abandoned the House of the Lord (2 Chron. 24:18). Another sad season had begun.

The House of Prayer was again restored in Hezekiah's day. The Chronicler testified about Hezekiah that "He did right in the sight of the LORD, according to all that his father David had done" (2 Chron. 29:2). His father Ahaz had done great evil in the land, and Hezekiah had to reopen the temple, repair its doors, clean house, and recommission the Levites. "My sons, do not be negligent now, for the LORD has chosen you to stand before Him, to minister to Him, and to be His ministers and burn incense" (2 Chron. 29:11). It was time to *sharath* (minister to) the Lord. The temple was cleansed, and sacrifices were reinstituted. "He then stationed the Levites in the House of the Lord with cymbals, with harps, and with lyres, according to the command of David and of Gad the king's seer, and of Nathan the prophet; for the command was from the LORD through His prophets" (2 Chron. 29:25). Revival came just in time. Assyria had overrun the northern kingdom. It would later take the main cities of Judah, and Jerusalem itself would be under siege.

Hezekiah fell ill. The prophet Isaiah came to tell him that it was time to get his house in order, but Hezekiah cried out to the Lord, whereupon God added fifteen years to his life. Manasseh, his son, was born in this period and was twelve years old when he became king (2 Chron. 33:1). He was arguably the worst king Judah ever had and more than any other king set the table for the Babylonian invasion. It was a very dark time for Judah, but God brought yet another invitation to national repentance in the days of Josiah.

Josiah was eight years old when he began his reign. His grandfather Manasseh and his father Amon were both terrible men. It is hard to imagine a worse upbringing. Amazingly, at the age of sixteen, Josiah began to seek the God of his father David. At the age of twenty, he purged Judah of all its graven images and altars. Six years later, he heard God's instructions through Shaphan, the secretary, who read the book of the Law of Moses to him. Josiah had been seeking faithfully, acted on what he knew and waited for God to reveal more to him. He responded further and pursued God more fervently. Josiah experienced delay before the Lord gave him the full instruction. He was like Moses, Samuel, and David. When added insight came, he pressed in further.

> Prepare *yourselves* by your fathers' households in your divisions, according to the writing of David king of Israel and according to the writing of his son Solomon … The singers, the sons of Asaph, *were* also at their stations according to the command of David, Asaph, Heman, and Jeduthun the king's seer; and the gatekeepers at each gate did not have to depart from their service, because the Levites their brethren prepared for them. (2 Chron. 35:4, 15)

Shaphan must have provided all of David's instructions as well as the book of the Law of Moses. The House of Prayer was revitalized. Passover was celebrated. The Chronicler commented that such a celebration had not occurred in Israel since the time of Samuel.

The House of Prayer had been restored when Israel was on the verge of national collapse and destruction with Jehoshaphat, Joash, Hezekiah, and now Josiah. Unfortunately, it was not many years before the Babylonian invasion. It appeared that once Josiah was gone, the House of Prayer also stopped. The people were eventually removed from the land for seventy years. This has been the unfortunate pattern for the people of God. It would have been better to give themselves to the House of Prayer first before being forced to do so.

The prophets aided Hezekiah's focus. Isaiah prophesied during the reign of Hezekiah and his insights and revelations were powerful. He would continue and even add to God's conversation on the nature of the House of the Lord—the House of Prayer.

Chapter Twelve

ISAIAH

I saiah wrote some 300 years after David. The House of Prayer had begun to fall apart perhaps even during the reign of Solomon. Its history was very much up-and-down, though mostly down. It reflected the spiritual climate of the nation. Isaiah was given a startling, heavenly revelation of the throne room in the temple, and God sent him to prophesy to Judah.

> He said, Go, and tell this people: "Keep on listening, but do not perceive; Keep on looking, but do not understand.' Render the hearts of this people insensitive, Their ears dull, And their eyes dim, Otherwise they might see with their eyes, Hear with their ears, Understand with their hearts, And return and be healed." (Isa. 6:9-10)

If Isaiah puzzled over the outcome of such a prophecy, his thoughts were not written down. How would Israel *sharath* the Lord if it were rendered blind and deaf? Isaiah provided very graphic detail on Israel's condition later in his book. An excerpt is as follows.

> Behold, the LORD'S hand is not so short
> That it cannot save; Nor is His ear so dull
> That it cannot hear. But your iniquities have
> made a separation between you and your
> God, And your sins have hidden His face
> from you so that He does not hear. For your
> hands are defiled with blood And your fin-
> gers with iniquity; Your lips have spoken
> falsehood, Your tongue mutters wickedness.
> No one sues righteously and no one pleads
> honestly. They trust in confusion and speak
> lies; They conceive mischief and bring forth
> iniquity. (Isa. 59:1-4)

The full indictment is much longer and just as graphic. The indictment was true, but where was the promise? How would Israel survive? If Israel didn't survive, what would become of the rest of the world? Isaiah laments, "We were pregnant, we writhed in labor, We gave birth, as it seems, only to wind. We could not accomplish deliverance [yeshuah] for the earth, Nor were inhabitants of the world born" (Isa. 26:18). Abraham's promises were clearly at risk. Only divine intervention would save the day.

God provided this sad commentary: "And He saw that there was no man, And was astonished that there was no one to intercede; Then His own arm brought salvation to Him, And His righteousness upheld Him" (Isa. 59:16). Moses had interceded for the nation of Israel. David had interceded for

Israel and Jerusalem. Now there was no one. There would be no peace in Jerusalem as David desired. His command concerning the House of Prayer was neglected. There would be no change unless God acted.

God continued His dialogue with Isaiah and then gave a stunning promise. "A throne will even be established in lovingkindness, And a judge will sit on it in faithfulness *in the tent of David*; Moreover, he will seek justice And be prompt in righteousness" (Isa. 16:5). A future day was on the way. The image of David's tent (*ohel*) affirmed God's accessibility, His *sharath*ing, and His desired leadership style—just like David. Isaiah's word further confirmed that David's tent did not operate like the temple or even Moses' tent of meeting where there was clear separation and hiddenness (temple area, courts, Holy Place, and Holy of Holies). Isaiah did not call this the *mishkan* or *succoth* but the simple *ohel* of David. The seat of the future government—its king and His throne—would be in the place of night and day prayer and worship—the *sharath* of the Lord— the sacrificial service *to* the Master from a forgiven, cleansed, humble, faithful and intimate heart generating the remarkable, delightful and deeply satisfying experience *of* the Master. In the fullness of that day, there would be no waiting and no delays. Justice would be prompt. It would be the high court of the land.

The Bridegroom God who commanded Isaiah to render Israel deaf and blind still had hope and was waiting.

> Therefore the LORD longs to be gracious
> to you, And therefore He waits on high to
> have compassion on you. For the LORD is
> a God of justice; How blessed are all those

who long for Him. O people in Zion, inhabitant in Jerusalem, you will weep no longer. He will surely be gracious to you at the sound of your cry; when He hears it, He will answer you. (Isa. 30:18-19)

God longed to be gracious. He would do all He could, but He waited for the sound of their cry in the temple courts as He told Solomon He would. He waited for the humble confession and the sacrifice of praise that came from broken and contrite hearts. For a short season, it did come with Hezekiah, but was quickly lost again under Manasseh.

Hezekiah had restored the House of Prayer and celebrated Passover with great heart. God responded through the prophet. "You will have songs as in the night when you keep the festival, And gladness of heart as when one marches to *the sound* of the flute, To go to the mountain of the LORD, to the Rock of Israel" (Isa. 30:29). Since Hezekiah moved according to the command of David, the night watch would have been reintroduced as well as the other elements of Davidic worship and intercession. God promised there would be songs of intercession in the night! Hezekiah's restoration of the night watch proved to be timely as the Assyrian army prepared to besiege Jerusalem.

The writer of the book of Kings tells us the Assyrian army was struck at *night*, killing 185,000 troops (2 Kgs. 19:35). Isaiah provided the following thunderous statement.

For at the voice of the LORD Assyria will
be terrified, *When* He strikes with the rod.
And every blow of the rod of punishment,

> Which the LORD will lay on him, Will be
> with *the music* of tambourines and lyres;
> And in battles, brandishing weapons, He
> will fight them. (Isa. 30:31-32)

The punishment of Assyria came with the House of
Prayer music of tambourines and lyres during the night
watch! When the king of Assyria awoke, his army was gone,
and he quickly departed for home. God's government works
at night, too! Retaking the night watch is inconvenient, but
impressive in its impact.

God spoke to Isaiah and emphasized His perspective on
David, and by implication Davidic worship. God wanted to
make it perfectly clear.

> Incline your ear and come to Me. Listen
> that you may live; And I will make an ever-
> lasting covenant with you, *According to* the
> faithful mercies shown to David. Behold,
> I have made him a witness to the peoples,
> A leader and commander for the peoples.
> (Isa. 55:3-4)

Isaiah provided a surprising and astonishing description
of David. Not only was he the standard for kings but he was
also a witness or testimony (LXX *marturion*) to the people as
well. His passionate pursuit of the House of Prayer and 24/7
Davidic intercessory worship, his failures and restoration,
and his continuing pursuit afterward, his time, treasure, and
talent were all a testimony. God's promise and direction are
not changed. Do it like David. He is the example, the witness

from God, a king with the priestly role of *sharath*ing the Lord. Incline your ear. Listen.

Modeling the life of David did not take root. As noted in the previous chapter, Hezekiah's revival was short. Manasseh was just around the corner and the people's sin was much deeper and grievous. God provided Isaiah with yet another profound revelation.

> Also the foreigners who join themselves to the LORD, To minister to Him, and to love the name of the LORD, To be His servants, everyone who keeps from profaning the Sabbath, And holds fast My covenant; Even those I will bring to My holy mountain, And make them joyful in My House of Prayer. Their burnt offerings and their sacrifices will be acceptable on My altar; For My house will be called a House of Prayer for all the peoples. (Isa. 56:6-7)

Certainly, Israel was in no condition to minister to the Lord. This would certainly have weighed heavily on Isaiah's heart. He had prophesied their blindness. Not surprisingly, God had a plan. He would bring *foreigners* and eunuchs — those previously excluded from God's presence — to minister to Him. They would *sharath* the Lord. This is staggering! It was what Joseph did that released such trust in his Egyptian masters. It was what Aaron did in the tabernacle (Ex. 28:35). It was what the Levites did (Num. 1:50). "For the LORD your God has chosen him and his sons from all your tribes, to stand and serve in the name of the LORD forever" (Deut.

18:5). It was what Samuel did before the Ark (1 Sam. 2:11). It was what happened in David's tent (1 Chron. 6:32). It was what Asaph was charged to do (1 Chron. 16:4). The table had now been set for another major shift in ministering to the Lord. In essence, foreigners, Gentiles, those with no standing in Israel, would become like Levites and *sharath* the Lord. Unthinkable.

The Lord had several more surprises for Isaiah. The fundamental, foundational characteristic or description of God's House was *prayer*—in the face of the Lord, 24/7, with intercession and worship as David, the divine witness (Isa. 55:4), had taught the people. Breathtaking. David's time, treasure, and talent went into the House of Prayer. David's priority, his passion was truly aligned with God's.

It might be tempting to see Isaiah's description of the House of Prayer as temporary and related only to the temple and Israel. However, Isaiah used an imperfect verb—continuing action into the future. He saw no end to the House of Prayer. Similarly, David had the expectation of being in the House of the Lord forever. And this was the experience of the heavenly host. There would be no end. The revelation of the House of Prayer would continue to unfold over time.

God dropped the next bombshell: The House of Prayer would be for all the peoples (LXX *ethnos*). God's House had a missions outreach mandate as David had written in Psalm 65! God wanted to draw the nations to come before His face. Though Israel had failed to reach the world, God would not fail. But there was more. *For all* is a Hebrew particle conjunction that can be translated in several ways: to, toward, for, belong to, *by*. Moses wrote, "It is a night to be observed for the LORD for having brought them out from the land of Egypt; this night is for the LORD, to be observed *by* all the sons of Israel throughout their generation." (Ex. 12:42). Solomon in his dedication prayer said, "whatever prayer or supplication is made by any man or *by all* Your people Israel, each knowing the affliction of his own heart, and spreading his hands toward this house" (1 Kgs. 8:38). The same Hebrew construction was used in the two previous passages as was used in Isaiah 56:7. The Septuagint translation can also be rendered *by all* (Jer. 8:3).

Isaiah made it clear that foreigners would *sharath* the Lord. Taken together, it is plausible to see the House of Prayer as for them and *by* them. Another piece of the House of Prayer puzzle may have been laid down. Foreigners would have to drive the House of Prayer alone during Israel's blindness, but they would benefit as well. Israel's unfaithfulness would not destroy God's plans. He could and would bring others near.

God was going to let foreigners come near to minister to Him (Isa. 56:6). These very ones Israel thought were excluded would end up having a desire for God and be brought close to the Lord. Isaiah may have wondered, "What would become of Israel?" God had a plan for that, too. He gave Isaiah a look into the future.

"For behold, darkness will cover the earth, And deep darkness the peoples; But the LORD will rise upon you, And His glory will appear upon you. And nations will come to your light, And kings to the brightness of your rising" (Isa. 60:2-3). Darkness was coming to the entire earth. Jew and Gentile (foreigner) would experience it. God's glory would rise upon Zion and Jacob. The rise was like the dawn. The beginning of the dawn is very small. The watchmen scan the horizon for its coming. The darkness begins to recede and the light ascends. It grows slowly to a crescendo of brightness. The earth begins to warm and is finally hot, bathed in a full blanket of warming light. The nations would be drawn to the dawning light. Isaiah was ecstatic.

> For Zion's sake I will not keep silent, And for Jerusalem's sake I will not keep quiet, Until her righteousness goes forth like brightness, And her salvation like a torch that is burning. The nations will see your righteousness, And all kings your glory; And you will be called by a new name Which the mouth of the LORD will designate. (Isa. 62:1-2)

Isaiah would not keep silent. He would proclaim Jerusalem's coming recovery. Isaiah didn't discuss his personal questions at this point, but God seemed to understand Isaiah's concern for Israel. God shared His plans with Isaiah.

God provided His four-point strategy before the end of the age would come.

> It will no longer be said to you, Forsaken, Nor to your land will it any longer be said, Desolate; But you will be called, My delight is in her, And your land, Married; For the LORD delights in you, And *to Him* your land will be married. For *as* a young man marries a virgin, *So* your sons will marry you; And as the bridegroom rejoices over

the bride, *So* your God will rejoice over you.
(Isa. 62:4-5)

Step One: He would release and emphasize His Bridegroom desire for His people, and God's sons would respond. They would become faithful and devoted. Since this was not the picture of Israel that Isaiah recognized, God added Step Two.

> On your walls, O Jerusalem, I have appointed watchmen; All day and all night they will never keep silent. You who remind the LORD, take no rest for yourselves; And give Him no rest until He establishes And makes Jerusalem a praise in the earth.
> (Isa. 62:6-7)

The intimacy of verses 4 and 5 would lead to day and night intercession as David had modeled. They were commanded to give God no rest until He made Jerusalem a praise in all the earth. Isaiah connected the dots. What Israel could not do for themselves, God would begin to do through His foreigners (Isa. 56). They would follow the testimony (witness) of David. They would be intercessors who would cry out day and night with abandon for the recovery of Jacob, themselves, and their nations. Intercession would be by them and for them. They too would find a home for the *Mighty One of Jacob*, just as David had done. What would be true of Jerusalem in an ultimate sense would be true in some measure for their own communities that needed God's light and salvation.

> The LORD has sworn by His right hand
> and by His strong arm, I will never again
> give your grain *as* food for your enemies;
> Nor will foreigners drink your new wine,
> for which you have labored. But those who
> garner it will eat it, and praise the LORD;
> And those who gather it will drink it in the
> courts of My sanctuary. Go through, go
> through the gates; Clear the way for the
> people; Build up, build up the highway;
> Remove the stones, lift up a standard over
> the peoples. (Isa. 62:8-10)

Step Three: God would release provision. God would lift up His right hand, sending His servants to go through, clear the way, build up, remove stones, and lift up a standard for the peoples. Jacob's sons and all the nations would be affected by God's strong arm. It would be like the dawn—steadily growing. God still had controversy with His son Jacob and with all the opposing nations that would need to be worked out, but the big picture was clear. The Bridegroom God was drawing His bride, providing her with escape from darkness (natural and spiritual), Jew and Gentile, into His light in powerful ways.

Then the final act of natural history, Step Four, would occur: God would move against His enemies. Isaiah saw it coming:

> Why is Your apparel red, And Your gar-
> ments like the one who treads in the wine
> press? I have trodden the wine trough alone,

128

> And from the peoples there was no man
> with Me. I also trod them in My anger And
> trampled them in My wrath; And their life-
> blood is sprinkled on My garments, And I
> stained all My raiment. For the day of ven-
> geance was in My heart, And My year of
> redemption has come. (Isa. 63:2-4)

The final Bridegroom action would not be an antiseptic event. It would be bloody. God would deal decisively with His enemies. He would free His Bride, so she would be His alone.

God would restore the fortunes of Zion. They would have a garland of praise instead of ashes (Isa. 61:3). They would have the oil of gladness, a mantle of praise, and be the planting of the Lord. Strangers would pasture Zion's flocks. "But you will be called the priests of the LORD; You will be spoken of *as* ministers of our God. You will eat the wealth of nations, And in their riches you will boast" (Isa. 61:6).

Isaiah was shown amazing things. God had a plan to restore Israel through the House of Prayer. It would be driven by Gentiles who would be brought near to *sharath* the Lord. In the season of Israel's blindness, the Gentiles who loved the Lord would cry out for her salvation. Through their intercession, Israel would once again become like David and *sharath* the Lord. A future king would sit in David's tent, dispensing righteousness. He would be of David's line and have David's heart for intercessory worship.

Isaiah set the tone for the House of Prayer. Other prophets would continue to fill out the picture of God's House of Prayer that was unfolding.

Chapter Thirteen

THE OTHER
PRE-EXILIC PROPHETS

A mos ministered approximately fifty years before Isaiah. He was sent to the northern kingdom of Israel to announce its fast-approaching judgment. Hezekiah would see the destruction of the northern kingdom and come close to losing Judah as well. Davidic practice was restored, and Judah was delivered for a time. Amos had many messages to deliver, but two are significant in considering the House of Prayer.

The first message was around a unique famine that will come in the last days. It will become nearly impossible to hear the Word of the Lord.

> Behold, days are coming, declares the Lord GOD, When I will send a famine on the land, Not a famine for bread or a thirst for water, But rather for hearing the words of the LORD. People will stagger from sea to sea And from the north even to the east; They will go to and fro to seek the word

of the LORD, But they will not find it.
(Amos 8:11-12)

There is no lack of scripture availability in Israel today or among the Western nations. Apart from the truly despotic nations or unreached people groups, the scriptures are accessible to most. The famine will not be a lack of scripture or truth speakers. Rather, it will be a famine of hearing. The underlying issue is simple—no heart to obey and therefore no ears to hear. The impact will be profound in the last days.

The House of Prayer will be a place of refuge, and as David noted, "In Your light we see light" (Ps. 36:9). Hearing and seeing will be possible in the House of Prayer, where declarations, songs, and intercession for God's commandments, statutes, and judgments occur. The widespread famine will not affect the House of Prayer where seeking saints with burning hearts are building their testimonies before the face of the Lord and one another.

The second message had to do with the fallen booth of David.

> In that day I will raise up the fallen booth of David, And wall up its breaches; I will also raise up its ruins And rebuild it as in the days of old; That they may possess the remnant of Edom And all the nations who are called by My name, Declares the LORD who does this. (Amos 9:11-12)

Amos spoke of the fallen *booth* or *sukkah* that will be raised up or restored. The restoration Amos saw has dynastic

(David) and hence governmental and territorial implications. Rebuilding will occur so that Israel *might take possession or dispossess* (strong militant terms) *the remnant of Edom and the rest of the nations*. Its militant nature is reminiscent of Psalm 2. Israel, with its Davidic king, will rule the nations and certainly its neighbors. It will no longer be the victim as it was under Assyria. Since it is impossible to separate David from the House of Prayer, the restoration of David's booth has a dimension of the House of Prayer in view. Further clarity comes from Luke and will be discussed in Chapter Sixteen.

Two significant implications can be drawn from Amos's word. First, restoration will occur in the last of the last days. In the following verses, God declared the general time period for this great work.

> Behold, days are coming, declares the LORD, "When the plowman will overtake the reaper And the treader of grapes him who sows seed; When the mountains will drip sweet wine And all the hills will be dissolved. Also I will restore the captivity of My people Israel, And they will rebuild the ruined cities and live *in them;* They will also plant vineyards and drink their wine, And make gardens and eat their fruit. I will also plant them on their land, And they will not again be rooted out from their land Which I have given them," Says the LORD your God. (Amos 9:14-15)

The greater David (Jesus) has come, but the dawning of the full release of Amos's word will be tied to the end of natural history and tied to Israel. Consequently, the restoration of the fallen booth of David was not intended to be a focus of the saints down through the centuries. It was for the end. Second, there is no need for restoration if David's booth is fully functional. It isn't. His earthly government is not in place. His kingdom territory is not in place, and his greatest longing, the House of Prayer, is not in place. Hence, it must be restored. There is no need to restore what might be replaced or rendered obsolete in the future. However, God does intend to restore it in the last days. It will be needed. It has value and significance for that season. Intervention will be needed, and that season is beginning to unfold now. Amos was not given the details of the steps to that unfolding House of Prayer drama. He was only given the promise.

Micah appears to have been a contemporary of Isaiah. He saw a slice of the coming kingdom (Mic. 4:1-2). He saw what the House of the Lord will be like. The mountain of the Lord will be the chief mountain. The nations will stream to the house of the God of Jacob to learn about God's ways and walk in His paths. He saw the Word of the Lord going forth from Zion. God will dispense justice from that mountain. God's words and His testimonies will be powerful and dominant. He will judge between many peoples. His throne will be in David's tent (Isa. 16:5).

One hundred years after Isaiah, the prophet Jeremiah would see several snapshots of the future. One in particular has similarities to what Isaiah saw. During the last days, he saw Israel — a great company — returning home, weeping and praying.

> For thus says the LORD, Sing aloud with
> gladness for Jacob, And shout among the
> chief of the nations; Proclaim, give praise
> and say, 'O LORD, save Your people, The
> remnant of Israel.' ... With weeping they
> will come, And by supplication I will lead
> them; I will make them walk by streams of
> waters, On a straight path in which they will
> not stumble; For I am a father to Israel, And
> Ephraim is My firstborn. (Jer. 31:7-9)

The House of Prayer is not mentioned here directly. However, singing, proclamation, and praise, as well as intercession with weeping and intimacy, are certainly House of Prayer attributes. Corporate, public intercession will be a significant source of supply in the natural and in the supernatural (revelation of the person of God and His plans), just as they had been for David. There will be provision—streams in the desert. There will be revelation—straight paths to follow that will not cause stumbling. The Father's heart, intimacy, will be revealed—Israel will know their Father. Their firstborn status and experience will be restored.

The Lord asked Jeremiah a rhetorical question surrounding God's promises.

> Thus says the LORD, 'If you can break My
> covenant for the day and My covenant for
> the night, so that day and night will not be
> at their appointed time, then My covenant
> may also be broken with David My servant
> so that he will not have a son to reign on his

throne, and with the Levitical priests, My ministers.' (Jer. 33:20-21)

The rhetorical question requires a *no* answer. Jeremiah knows there will be a House of Prayer. The covenant with David will not be broken, and God's Levitical priests will *sharath* the Lord. God will have foreign (wild olive) and Jewish (native olive) Levites who have this assignment to *sharath* the greater David, Jesus. It is a promise He will keep.

Joel, a likely contemporary of Jeremiah, provided an important context for the future House of Prayer. He was commanded to blow a trumpet in Zion, sound an alarm (Joel 2:1), and proclaim a solemn assembly. The people needed to gather, to rend their hearts, not their garments, and consecrate a fast. The priests needed to weep between the porch and the altar. Business as usual activity had to stop. It was a 2 Chronicles 7:14 call. Intercession was needed. "Who knows whether He will *not* turn and relent And leave a blessing behind Him, *Even* a grain offering and a drink offering For the LORD your God?" (Joel 2:14)

Sadly, there was no response in Joel's day. Jerusalem was destroyed by the Babylonians.

Amos saw the coming season of Israel's recovery. It would occur in the last days during a time of heightened anxiety. The Word of the Lord would be scarce, and many would search for it. But God will break through. The trumpet will sound. Solemn assemblies (Joel 2:15) will be called, with weeping and fasting. God will establish His house as the highest in the land, and the nations will stream to it. Israel will return in a spirit of supplication and find intimacy waiting to lead them. God will not renege on His promise to David or His promise to the Levitical singers. There will be *sharath*.

The natural timeline of the House of Prayer continued after Jerusalem was destroyed. Jeremiah's seventy years were fulfilled. The remnant returned. The heart for a House of Prayer among the returnees was not dead. God is still building our understanding of His House of Prayer.

Chapter Fourteen

POST-EXILIC TIMES

B y the time Ezra wrote (440 BC), the Ark appeared to be missing, and Solomon's temple was long gone. Zerubbabel had laid the foundation of a new temple (536 BC), but problems for the returnees arose immediately. Priorities were wrong. Haggai gave the remnant God's message.

> Thus says the LORD of hosts, 'This people says, "The time has not come, *even* the time for the house of the LORD to be rebuilt." Then the word of the LORD came by Haggai the prophet, saying, "Is it time for you yourselves to dwell in your pan-eled houses while this house *lies* desolate?" Now therefore, thus says the LORD of hosts, "Consider your ways! You have sown much, but harvest little; *you* eat, but *there is* not *enough* to be satisfied; *you* drink, but *there is* not *enough* to become drunk; *you* put on clothing, but no one is warm *enough*; and he who earns, earns wages *to put* into a

> purse with holes." Thus says the LORD of
> hosts, "Consider your ways!" (Hag. 1:2-7)

During the construction of the second temple, Haggai posed his telling question. They focused on their personal needs and convenience rather than the construction of the temple and restoration of its ultimate function—the House of Prayer. What little was harvested was not enough. This lack and loss applied to all areas of their lives. *Consider your ways* was the prophetic correction given to Israel. Isaiah called God's House a *House of Prayer*. David was the premier example, and a witness to the people (Isa.55:4). Night and day worship was God's heart for His house. The House of Prayer was to be the great priority and the saints in Haggai's day were not giving it the attention warranted.

The people received the correction. Reconstruction continued. It was not enough that the altar of sacrifice had been built and was now in use (Ezra. 3:2). House of Prayer elements needed to be in place. There would be a time when the House of Prayer would function without temple or Ark, priest or Levite, and eventually without Jerusalem or even Israel! That season was still in the future.

> Now when the builders had laid the founda-
> tion of the temple of the LORD, the priests
> stood in their apparel with trumpets, and
> the Levites, the sons of Asaph, with cym-
> bals, to praise the LORD according to the
> directions of King David of Israel. And
> they sang, praising and giving thanks to
> the LORD, *saying*, For He is good, for His

> lovingkindness is upon Israel forever. And
> all the people shouted with a great shout
> when they praised the LORD because the
> foundation of the House of the Lord was
> laid. (Ezra 3:10-11)

House of Prayer operations are mentioned in the description of the foundation ceremony. It isn't clear if the full 24/7 was implied or whether it was simply the Davidic support for sacrifices provided in 1 Chronicles 16:39. Given Haggai's and Zechariah's awareness of the consequences of Israel's past disobedience and their grasp of God's prophetic instructions, it is likely that 24/7 in some dimension was being practiced.

Almost eighty years later, on the eve of Ezra's return to Jerusalem (458 BC), he discovered that those who *sharath*ed the Lord were missing (Ezra 8:15). He sent messengers to Iddo "the leading man at the place Casiphia; and I told them what to say to Iddo *and* his brothers, the temple servants at the place Casiphia, *that is,* to bring ministers to us for the house of our God" (Ezra 8:17). Apparently, those Israelites left in Babylon up to this time continued to train and equip temple servants who would *sharath* (minister to) God. Ezra had the priests and people arranged and ready to return to Israel but needed the Levitical singers. He would not leave without them. It was that important.

After Ezra arrived in Israel, he prayed before the congregation and provided fascinating insights into God's House of Prayer. He had Solomon's 2 Chronicles 7:14 words, David's words (Ps. 55:8-17), and Amos's declaration in mind.

> But now for a brief moment grace has
> been *shown* from the LORD our God, to
> leave us an escaped remnant and to give
> us a peg in His holy place, that our God
> may enlighten our eyes and grant us a little
> reviving in our bondage. For we are slaves;
> yet in our bondage our God has not forsaken
> us, but has extended lovingkindness to us in
> the sight of the kings of Persia, to give us
> reviving to raise up the house of our God,
> to restore its ruins and to give us a wall in
> Judah and Jerusalem. (Ezra 9:8-9)

The second temple had been built and was operating. Restoring its ruin is an echo of Amos's promise (Amos 9:11-13), with particular emphasis on God's House. The desire to see the restoration of a strong national Israel along with its Davidic king was certainly there. But the first priority for restoration was God's House (Isa. 56:7)—in essence, David's tent, his experience, and approach to worship, which had fallen and lay in ruins both figuratively and literally.

Giving a wall in Judah is likely a spiritual application. The walls around the city were still broken down and its gates burned by fire. The actual city wall wouldn't be fixed for another twelve years, when Nehemiah arrived. When David confessed his sin with Bathsheba and sought restoration, he asked God to build the wall of Jerusalem (Ps. 51:18). He understood what his sin had done. The physical wall in David's time was not affected, but the more significant spiritual wall had been damaged. God spoke to Ezekiel some years before Ezra and told Ezekiel He could not find one man who would build up the wall and stand in the gap to intercede and avert judgment (Ezek. 22:30).

For Ezra, the wall of intercession was located in the city of Jerusalem. It would make no sense to build a physical wall for all of Judah. But a spiritual wall for Judah would make perfect sense. Jerusalem's surrounding territory would be impacted and managed with a spiritual wall as Jehoshaphat had discovered. Ezra understood this spiritual principle. He wanted the House of Prayer back.

This promise for a *wall* may be an allusion to what the House of Prayer brings to the table. Sin weakens and removes the wall, exposing the city to greater levels of evil and temptation. In Israel's case, the failed wall was both natural—defeated and exiled for seventy years in Babylon—and spiritual—no Davidic intercessory worship with all its benefits. There were no prophetic watchmen on the wall to keep the city in good repair; none to look into the city; none to hold the gates; none to look outward from the wall (Isa. 62:6); and no one standing in God's courts to challenge evil or promote righteousness. God told Isaiah days were coming when He would put intercessors on the wall to cry out night and day for Jerusalem (Isa. 61-62). The outcome would be glorious.

Ironically, being unequally yoked (Ezra 9:1-2) was top of the list of sins Ezra addressed. Those assembled heard the message and trembled. Unconfessed sin was another invitation to slavery. Israel and the world needed the House of Prayer. Ezra gave thanks for the wall God was giving again. Nehemiah would have more to say on this issue of the wall.

The *peg* may have been a sign of permanence (Isa. 54:2), but it was also reminiscent of David's tent. It was a simple structure and would have required pegs in the beginning. And it held the Ark and was located in Jerusalem. Moses's tabernacle operated out of a tent with pegs, but never made it out of Gibeon.

Nehemiah (445 B.C.) heard the report of Jerusalem's burned gates, recognized a facet of Israel's problem, and followed Solomon's 2 Chronicles 7:14 prayer.

> They said to me, The remnant there in the province who survived the captivity are in great distress and reproach, and the wall of Jerusalem is broken down and its gates are burned with fire ... let Thine ear now be attentive and Thine eyes open to hear the prayer of Thy servant which I am praying before Thee now, day and night, on behalf of the sons of Israel Thy servants, confessing the sins of the sons of Israel which we have sinned against Thee; I and my father's house have sinned. (Neh. 1:1:3, 6)

Nehemiah clearly expected God to react in accordance with the prayer approach Solomon laid out. The House of Prayer and vertical worship ascended in some measure with Ezra, but an important element was missing. Jerusalem's wall and its gates had been burned with fire. The city of Jerusalem was exposed to God's enemies. God heard Nehemiah's prayer. His favor was upon Nehemiah, and King Artaxerxes sent him back to Jerusalem to repair the wall—all expenses paid. He came to Israel in the twentieth year of King Artaxerxes. Once the walls and gates had been restored, Nehemiah, governor of Israel, was able to regulate commerce and protect the purposes of God for Jerusalem. The Jewish way of life, the Sabbath and festivals could be secured (Neh. 10:31). Those who opposed Israel's way of life could be restrained. The natural wall and gate reveal and illustrate important aspects of the spiritual wall and gate God wants.

Cyrus allowed Zerubbabel and the Jews to return. The enemies of God were not happy with a restored temple. "Then the people of the land discouraged the people of Judah, and frightened them from building, and hired counselors against them to frustrate their counsel all the days of Cyrus king of Persia, even until the reign of Darius king of Persia" (Ezra 4:4-5).

Furthermore, the enemies of God were incensed and became truly adversarial when the wall was being repaired.

> Now when Sanballat, Tobiah, the Arabs, the Ammonites and the Ashdodites heard that the repair of the walls of Jerusalem went on, *and* that the breaches began to be closed, they were very angry. All of them conspired together to come *and* fight against Jerusalem and to cause a disturbance in it. (Neh. 4:7-8)

Worship was not appreciated by the natural enemies of God. Even more so, the saints could not be allowed to control the walls and gates. A functioning House of Prayer was bad news to the region. Intercession from the walls would control the gates, protect the city, promote righteousness and influence the region. It had to be stopped at all cost! The House of Prayer that *sharath*ed the Lord and owned the city walls and gates would be disastrous to the enemies of God.

Nehemiah did not discuss his plans immediately when he first arrived (Neh. 2:12, 445 BC). He operated under the radar for a short season. Sanballat the Horonite, Tobiah the Ammonite, and Geshem the Arab, the classic enemies of God (Neh. 2:19), vigorously opposed this work as expected. Almost everyone was engaged in rebuilding the wall once the plan became public. The priests, the Levites, officials, daughters (Neh. 3:12), and regular folks all lent a hand. Not all the nobles or leaders supported the work (Neh. 3:5). Opposition often comes from within as well as without. The status quo represents a powerful barrier to change. To admit the need for change and to pursue a course correction often implies fault at some level which stirs enmity. Returning to the ancient paths provokes hearts (Jer. 6:16). Amazingly, almost all the saints recognized the need for a secure wall and gates.

Opposition grew stronger as the work neared completion. A guard had to be set night and day. An attack could come at any time (Neh. 4:9), and probably not when it was convenient. Misappropriation of funds on the part of some of the leaders made it difficult for those who were laboring on the walls (Neh. 5:10), which necessitated correction and repentance. Funds needed to be allocated to the work of the House of Prayer. It was a costly endeavor. Nehemiah actually applied himself to the work on the wall (Neh. 5:16). It was not delegated to a task force. It required servant leadership.

The enemies of the wall tried to distract Nehemiah (Neh. 6:2-3) and intimidate him (Neh. 6:6). False prophetic words were given to cause fear and disengagement (Neh. 6:12-13). The true word of the Lord must stack up with scripture. Nehemiah understood the need for Jerusalem's gates and walls. He stayed focused. He would not give in to threats or intimidation.

Once the wall and gates were completed, Nehemiah organized the dedication of the completed wall. He gave instructions to the Levites, "to praise and give thanks, as prescribed by David the man of God, division corresponding to division" (Neh. 12:24). The Levites showed many of the ministry elements David had first entrusted to them in 1 Chronicles 16. There was praise, gladness and thanksgiving, remembrance (Neh. 9:5-9), declarations about who God is and His plans (Neh. 9:6), and songs and musical instruments (Neh. 12:27). David's commands were being followed.

Nehemiah left and returned to King Artaxerxes in Susa twelve years later to give a firsthand report. He was there for a time and then was granted leave to return to Israel, but in his absence, the House of Prayer began to unravel. Two events shaped this decline.

> Now prior to this, Eliashib the priest, who was appointed over the chambers of the house of our God, being related to Tobiah, had prepared a large room for him, where formerly they put the grain offerings, the frankincense, the utensils and the tithes of grain, wine and oil prescribed for the Levites, the singers and the gatekeepers, and the contributions for the priest. (Neh. 13:4-5)

Eliashib's son was unequally yoked (Neh. 13:28), which brought compromise to the family of God. Consequently, one of God's enemies was able to move into the storeroom used to supply the Levitical singers and support staff. The supplies moved out, and the enemy moved in. This may have triggered the second event. The singers had to return to their farms.

> I also discovered that the portions of the Levites had not been given *them*, so that the Levites and the singers who performed the service had gone away, each to his own field. So I reprimanded the officials and said, Why is the house of God forsaken? Then I gathered them together and restored them to their posts. All Judah then brought the tithe of the grain, wine, and oil into the storehouses. (Neh. 13:10-12)

The House of Prayer had a big challenge. It was expensive maintaining all the staff in 24/7 Davidic worship. The leaders, including Eliashib, chose to suspend the Levitical portion of support. True 24/7 worship stopped. The simpler Davidic support for the sacrifice schedule might have still functioned. This simpler sacrifice schedule would have made it easier for the singers to be bi-vocational. They could work their farms and still sing. But it was still a compromise. Regardless of the exact nature of the interruption, Nehemiah considered this to be forsaking the house. Davidic singers were critical—no singers, no 24/7 intercession, no spiritual wall. The enemy had a free hand in the city. Nehemiah had

Tobiah removed, and the Levitical provision and singers regathered.

God wanted a fully functional House of Prayer. When it became broken because of sin, He wanted confession, repentance, humility, and a turning-away from evil to get it restored. Once reestablished, it would release the full measure of its kingdom benefits to Israel and beyond. The king of Persia realized this fact. He wanted prayer for the well-being of his family and kingdom and knew where to get it. "For *there* was a commandment from the king concerning them and a firm regulation for the song leaders day by day" (Neh. 11:23). House of Prayer intercession was essential. Amazingly, the pagan government of the day understood and demanded it.

There may be many reasons why the Levitical singers were sent back to their farms. The House of Prayer was inconvenient, requiring travel to Jerusalem. A fully operational, day and night House of Prayer was invasive and hard on the lifestyle. Likewise, extravagant 24/7 worship and prayer required much financial support. Eliminating or reducing the singers reduced everyone's burden as well. Therefore, the best solution, outside of full obvious disobedience, was to follow David's instructions minimally. Fortunately, Nehemiah saw this differently. He would not forsake the House.

Malachi is the last of the post exilic books and the last book of the Old Testament. One aspect of his ministry makes no sense apart from what God is about to do.

> For from the rising of the sun even to its
> setting, My name *will be* great among the

> nations, and in every place incense is going
> to be offered to My name, and a grain
> offering *that is* pure; for My name *will be*
> great among the nations, says the LORD of
> hosts (Mal. 1:11).

Incense will be offered among the nations. It will not be exclusive to Jerusalem and the mount of the Lord! Presumably, it will no longer be an Aaron-only activity. Malachi looked ahead to a future time and saw incense (prayer)—an acceptable and pure gift—offered to the Lord. *Grain* is assumed by the translators. A better translation would be *incense, a tribute that is pure, will be offered in every place*. It will become the sacrifice of prayer, and it will be offered in *locations*, that is, in geographic *locations in the nations*. Presumably God would choose the locations as He did with Jerusalem. One wonders if the standing place, or location for offerings, will be in cities across the nations. In essence, David modeled a practice in Jerusalem—holding the walls and gates through intercessory worship—that would later be exported around the globe. Chapter Twenty-Two will further explore the coming of this Davidic practice to the cities of the earth.

This tremendous promise came after God complained to Malachi. "Oh that there were one among you who would shut the gates, that you might not uselessly kindle fire on My altar! I am not pleased with you," says the LORD of hosts, "nor will I accept an offering from you" (Mal. 1:10). God was not looking for an external *sharath* alone, but an internal heart of *sharath*ing. He would prefer to have no *sharath*ing if the heart was not involved. Yet God looked forward to a future season of Davidic worship as described in Mal 1:11.

Unfortunately, Israel believed God's presence was a magic button of provision. After all, He lived in Solomon's temple. They thought God's kind provision was a right of theirs even though they had no relationship with Him and did not seek Him. The prophets warned them not to believe the presence of the Ark would absolve them of their disobedience and rebellion (Jer. 7:4). The people couldn't and wouldn't grasp this message of the relational Bridegroom God. Ultimately, the temple, believed to contain Him, was destroyed, and the people were either killed or deported to Babylon. If Malachi was a contemporary of Nehemiah, as seems likely, then God's message on closing the gates, which He had already done once through Nebuchadnezzar, is sobering. Rome was just around the corner in time. He was willing to shut down one place of incense, even for a second time, while establishing other locations. God will have a pure tribute.

The House of Prayer is not mentioned as a functioning form of worship after Nehemiah. The restoration of the House of Prayer would be for another season. Fascinatingly, sacrifices without the House of Prayer continued into Jesus's day and beyond, until the temple was destroyed in AD70. Religious form without substance can have a long lifespan.

David may have seen a little of the future. He would declare, "O send out Your light and Your truth, let them lead me; Let them bring me to Your holy hill And to Your dwelling places" (Ps. 43:3). He used the plural *places*. Keil and Delitzsch calls this the "amplificative designation of the tent" (Keil and Delitzsch 1975, Continued, 61). It occurs in

Psalms 84:2 and 46:4. This may well be an emphatic description. Perhaps, however, this looks forward to a day when there really are *places* of His dwelling around the world. In that sense then, David was being prophetic and not poetic.

The prophetic last days accounts that have been included in this chapter and the previous chapter are helpful for at least two reasons. First, they provide God's intended outcome and are encouraging. Since He doesn't change, this outcome was in His heart when He spoke to Moses and later David. He would draw the nations. They would come to discover His ways and paths. The Levities would declare, sing, and intercede according to God's statutes and judgments. Foreigners, functioning as Levites, would come before the face of God and become part of His people (Rom. 9:25). They would learn to *sharath* Him. The House of Prayer would operate on the unseen city walls, blessing the city, holding the gates—looking inward and outward, gaining heavenly insight and fueling up the intercession in God's courts for God's kingdom business while frustrating the enemy's plans.

Second, the last days prophetic verses give warning. The House of Prayer is marvelous, but it is time-consuming, invasive, challenging to maintain, and if the singers and musicians are fully supported, expensive. Everyone gets stirred up: enemies and friends alike. Haggai saw the struggle of the people. He reminded them that they ended up losing more when they didn't follow the Lord. Restoring the temple and its practices was the first priority. Not all of Nehemiah's leaders were faithful. Some impeded or even derailed God's plans for His house. The temptation to compromise and grow lax is real. The promise of God means Israel will get there, but it won't be without bruises, as the warnings indicate. The Gentiles called to this mission should consider the promise and warning, too.

Because God's intentions have not yet been fulfilled, there will be a transition from where we are today to where God intends us to be. This transition has many dynamics, and a couple of those have been introduced. The New Testament marks a final installment on Davidic worship and will be considered next.

Chapter Fifteen

NEW TESTAMENT INTRODUCTION

T he New Testament period opens with the introduction of John the Baptist. Things are not good in Israel.

> "The beginning of the gospel of Jesus Christ, the Son of God. As it is written in Isaiah the prophet: "BEHOLD, I SEND MY MESSENGER AHEAD OF YOU, WHO WILL PREPARE YOUR WAY; 3 THE VOICE OF ONE CRYING IN THE WILDERNESS, 'MAKE READY THE WAY OF THE LORD, MAKE HIS PATHS STRAIGHT.'" John the Baptist appeared in the wilderness preaching a baptism of repentance for the forgiveness of sins (Mark 1:1-4).

The message comes in the wilderness and ominously, not in Jerusalem. John cries out for a baptism of repentance. The crowds come out to hear a radical message of recommitment in preparation for one who is coming. John saw the

Pharisees and Sadducees coming and warns them that the axe is already laid to the root (Matt. 3:10). The winnowing fork of judgment is in the hands of the one who is coming (Matt. 3:12). Why this strong warning to the leaders?

Religious leaders of Jesus's day did not wish to lose the level of control and influence they had over the people. They were reluctant to take a strong public stand, jeopardizing their position with Rome until convinced that armed rebellion against Roman domination would carry the day. Isolated personal prayer or formal ecclesiastical prayer was tolerable. A fully functional Davidic House of Prayer would never fly.

In 63 BC, the Roman general Pompey captured Jerusalem, bringing an end to Jewish control of their nation. By 37 BC, Herod the Great—of non-Jewish origin—was on the scene. He ruled Israel under Rome. He and his heirs were brutal and despotic. Jewish religious life was at a terrible low.

There were two main Jewish groups vying for supremacy. The Sadducees—aristocrats, the temple party who promoted the status quo—were duplicitous and interested in appeasement with Rome. They controlled the high priesthood and accepted only the Torah. All doctrines not obvious in the Torah were rejected. Theologically, they would have no interest in Davidic worship.

The Pharisees—party of the synagogue—emphasized personal piety with a desire to be recognized as such. They were Torah-centric but accepted all the Old Testament and were isolated and fiercely independent. Pharisees were practical but given to legalistic (controlling) observance. They were proud. The synagogue model gained dominance over time but had strict rules of adherence. Centralized Davidic worship, although theologically permissible, went against their independent instincts and would require humility as well as a closer relationship to the Sadducees. They too would have little interest in the House of Prayer.

Of several smaller parties, one should be mentioned. The Essenes had no interest in public religious observance. They were separate and encouraged strict legal observance. They believed temple worship was corrupt and therefore abandoned the temple. They lived in the wilderness, pursuing an apocalyptic outlook. With strict observance in their hearts and no clean temple, apocalyptic experience was all that was available. They had no interest in Jerusalem-based Davidic worship. A House of Prayer in the temple courts would not be possible.

Basically no one wanted the House of Prayer. Jesus was not received well by Israel. The rulers of the temple in Jesus's day and after His death and resurrection, did not embrace a Davidic style of worship nor would they have supported one. Pride held them captive (Acts 5:17). Those who considered themselves to be full were actually empty (1 Sam. 2:3-5). Jesus did not come as the expected Psalm 2 Messiah. "For even the Son of Man did not come to be served, but to serve, and to give His life a ransom for many" (Mark 10:45). This was Jesus's focus. Psalm 2 would come later. Restoration of the House of Prayer was, again, for another season.

Jesus said, "Do not think that I came to abolish the Law or the Prophets; I did not come to abolish but to fulfill" (Matt. 5:17). There is no New Testament command to abandon Davidic intercessory worship. There is also no indication that night and day prayer was ever fulfilled. Blood sacrifice for the remission of sins was fulfilled in Jesus and is no longer required. All foods are clean. Adultery and murder have been expanded to include what is done in the heart, and not simply when they occur in the flesh. There is clarification in the New Testament and continuity between the Old and New.

There is, also, no clear or unambiguous command made by Jesus or the apostles to fully implement the House of Prayer vision as a normative practice for the church. This may seem surprising, given this Old Testament survey on the House of Prayer. Acts 15 may hold part of the rationale for a formal silence on the topic and will be considered in the next chapter. Since the Old Testament did not disappear with Jesus, it may not have been necessary to repeat all the commands and promises that were still in effect. Jesus said, "until heaven and earth pass away, not the smallest letter or stroke shall pass from the Law until all is accomplished" (Matt. 5:18). None of His words will be lost. There will be an accounting for every one of them.

The New Testament, however, is not quiet about the House of Prayer. There is a strong Davidic undercurrent in most of the books. Jesus was and is a man of prayer. He is fully God and fully man, understanding how heaven runs, how the earth has run since the dawn of time, and how it will run in the future. He is fully familiar with Moses and David; God had given them both heavenly models to follow. When Jesus speaks, He speaks from the context and content of what God has already spoken. Jesus, Himself, is the Word and His words matter to Him and to those who love Him.

"Christ Jesus is He who died, yes, rather who was raised, who is at the right hand of God, who also intercedes for us" (Rom. 8:34). Intercession is not a new thing to Jesus. The writer of the book of Hebrews, when considering Jesus, gives us the following insight: "but Jesus, on the other hand, because He continues forever, holds His priesthood permanently. Therefore He is able also to save forever those who draw near to God through Him, since He always lives to make intercession for them" (Heb. 7:24-25). Jesus is a priest. He has drawn near to God and always lives to make intercession. This has always been His heart. His teaching on prayer has a rich and deep context. Captivatingly, He told John, "If anyone serves Me, he must follow Me; and where I am, there My servant will be also; if anyone serves Me, the Father will honor him" (John 12:26). Jesus is in the throne room praying today. Presumably, His servants are following His lead.

Prayer was a priority for the earthly Jesus, too. "In the early morning, while it was still dark, Jesus got up, left the house, and went away to a secluded place, and was praying there" (Mark 1:35). Jesus made the remarkable statement, "Truly, truly, I say to you, the Son can do nothing of Himself, unless it is something He sees the Father doing; for whatever the Father does, these things the Son also does in like manner" (John 5:19). And again, "For I did not speak on My own initiative, but the Father Himself who sent Me has given Me a commandment as to what to say and what to speak" (John 12:49). Jesus did not spell out the mechanism for such revelation and insight. It might turn out to be very simple. He prayed and His Father answered. David said, "in Your light we see light" (Ps. 36:9) —revelation— and he commanded his heart to seek the face of God (Ps. 27:8). The House of Prayer was the seedbed for this experience—night and day intercession and worship before God's face.

Ostentatious prayers are never a great idea in public or private. Jesus told His listeners to avoid doing this before men (Matt. 6:5-6). What should have been self-evident truth had to be commanded. They should get away to a private place where they could pray in secret to God who sees what is done in secret and rewards it. He told His listeners to gather together and agree in prayer (Matt. 18:19-20). He would join them in that prayer. Jesus did not distinguish between secret and corporate prayer. He expected both and still does.

In Jesus's day, there were devout men from every nation who were drawn to the Passover feast. The House of Prayer was not in operation at that time in Jerusalem, but men came as David said they would. Josephus, a Jewish historian from that period, suggested that as many as 2.5 million Jews were in Jerusalem for the feast. Unfortunately, the temple courts were being used to buy and sell goods rather than to offer prayer and engage with the Bridegroom God. Jesus was greatly angered by this.

> And He made a scourge of cords, and drove *them* all out of the temple, with the sheep and the oxen; and He poured out the coins of the money changers and overturned their tables; and to those who were selling the doves He said, Take these things away; stop making My Father's house a place of business. His disciples remembered that it was written, ZEAL FOR YOUR HOUSE WILL CONSUME ME. (John 2:15-17)

The disciples connected David's words surrounding the House of Prayer (Ps. 69:9) with what Jesus was doing.

Ignoring the original purpose for the House of Prayer, men were carrying out business in the temple where worshipers should have been able to stand and pray while the Levites *sharath*ed the Lord. These men were destroying the Father's purpose for His house (Isa. 56:7). In a rare display of anger, Jesus aggressively affirms God's longing for Davidic worship and prayer. It is interesting to note that the disciples' training and understanding of the scriptures immediately led them to David and his heart for the House of Prayer. This awakened and informed their desire for and practice of prayer in the days to come.

When the corporate House of Prayer dimension is added to the life of the saints, something powerful occurs. Jehoshaphat discovered potent deliverance as the House of Prayer singers began to minister to the Lord, and the armies invading Judah were crushed. Hezekiah discovered this as well. The Assyrian army was destroyed as the night watch sang! David enumerated the many blessings of the prayer room: mission to the nations, city strategy and defense: prosperity, confusing evil in the city, abundance, place of refuge—a hiding place, insight, intercessions for others, resource, and fellowship. And this may be a short list!

Davidic worship is no less critical than either personal prayer or small group prayer. Jesus made no attempt to tease out the unique contributions of each but endorsed all three and desired all of them. No one form of prayer was considered a substitute for the other two. Jesus wants them all.

The Bridegroom God had not changed. He was actively steering the events of the New Testament and setting up relational filters—speaking in parables and using difficult or dark sayings. Luke provided his readers the following summary of godly pursuit from the book of Acts.

> And the brethren immediately sent Paul and Silas away by night to Berea; and when they arrived, they went into the synagogue of the Jews. Now these were more noble-minded than those in Thessalonica, for they received the word with great eagerness, examining the Scriptures daily, to *see* whether these things were so. (Acts 17:10-11)

This is still the posture of the godly. "We want to study to see whether these things are so." The Bereans were commended. They didn't exaggerate, ignore, or marginalize what the scriptures taught. They didn't jump to conclusions but dug in and investigated (Acts 17:11). The gospel was hidden. Paul described the mystery of the gospel (Eph. 3:3-4) being revealed by him. What God intended in the gospel can certainly be seen retrospectively in the Old Testament, but understanding needed to await the death and resurrection of Jesus to complete the picture. It needed investigation, which the Bereans did. God's approach surprised them, as it had surprised Paul, and they needed to search the scriptures.

In a similar way, the House of Prayer was revealed to David, but its understanding and restoration awaited a last days season, as Amos had seen. The clarity around David's practice was obscured by time and circumstances. Thoughtful examination will be required to see what God is doing. A degree of hiddenness should be expected from the Bridegroom God. Elements of Davidic worship do exist in the New Testament record. The faithful believer must press forward to discover God's hidden things. With this as background, House of Prayer themes begin to emerge in the New Testament. We will start with the gospels and identify several Davidic worship elements. This is a starting place and not an exhaustive list.

> And there was a prophetess, Anna the daughter of Phanuel, of the tribe of Asher. She was advanced in years … and then as a widow to the age of eighty-four. And she never left the temple, serving night and day with fastings and prayers. And at that very moment she came up and *began* giving thanks to God, and continued to speak of Him to all those who were looking for the redemption of Jerusalem (Luke 2:36-38).

Anna was not a Levite but a layperson. She appeared to be a night and day saint serving in the temple courts, giving thanks. She spent the bulk of her life in prayer and fasting. She persevered in this Davidic lifestyle some sixty-plus years and she would not keep silent—just like Isaiah said (Isa. 62:6-7). Anna pressed the Lord daily for the redemption of Israel and declared God's coming salvation to all who would listen. She sounds very much like a Davidic worshiper who understood David's commands. No doubt, the authorities ignored her as a peculiar old woman. However, God was listening to those in the courts of His house and she was given the great joy of welcoming Jesus to His house!

The story of Jesus coming to the house of Martha and Mary is also instructive.

> She had a sister called Mary, who was seated at the Lord's feet, listening to His word. But Martha was distracted with all her preparations; and she came up *to Him* and said, "Lord, do You not care that my sister has left me to do all the serving alone? Then tell her to help me." But the Lord answered and said to her, "Martha, Martha, you are worried and bothered about so many things; but *only* one thing is necessary, for Mary has chosen the good part, which shall not be taken away from her (Luke 10:39-42).

Mary sat at the feet of Jesus, and He commended her choice in doing so, even though her sister Martha was working hard and had asked the Lord to redirect Mary to help out. Mary's *only one thing is necessary* would not be taken from her. Intimacy was Mary's focus even when family and cultural roles suggested she do otherwise. Like David, intimacy came first. If she had been able to visit the church in Ephesus in the book of Revelation, she could have offered the saints some valuable coaching. Jesus was also impressed by the woman faithfully seeking justice.

> Now He was telling them a parable to show that at all times they ought to pray and not to lose heart, saying, In a certain city there was a judge who did not fear God

and did not respect man... And the Lord said, Hear what the unrighteous judge said; now, will not God bring about justice for His elect who cry to Him day and night, and will He delay long over them? I tell you that He will bring about justice for them quickly. However, when the Son of Man comes, will He find faith on the earth (Luke 18:1-2, 6-8)?

In Luke 18:7, Jesus asked His listeners a hypothetical question. Would God delay? The expected answer was no, God would not delay long, and He did care about justice. The Bridegroom's heart is to restore what has been lost to its rightful place. Justice was a significant theme for David (2 Sam. 8:15) and would be a dominant concern in David's future tent (Isa. 16:5). Jesus gave the purpose of the parable in the introduction. It was about always praying and not giving up. Praying is an *at-all-times* activity or, as Jesus put it, day and night. Perseverance is required in faithful prayer. Hence, the admonition to not lose heart. Follow David's example.

Commentators are drawn to the theme of delayed answers to prayer, which is a great challenge in the body of Christ and a reminder of the need to persevere (waiting under adversity). It may well be that Jesus was giving a clue about prayer when He used the phrase *day and night*. Jesus was well aware of how this phrase had been used in the Old Testament. It is what God expected. This is a much more invasive lifestyle of prayer than most saints, individually or collectively, are prepared to pursue. This may be part of the reason for delayed answers—little perseverance. Prayer is not vain repetition, nor is it a simple request never repeated. It requires perseverance. "You who remind the LORD, take no rest for yourselves" (Isa. 62:6). God doesn't need reminding.

Jesus followed up the story of the persistent widow with two men coming to the temple to pray.

> Two men went up into the temple to pray, one a Pharisee and the other a tax collector. "The Pharisee stood and was praying this to himself: 'God, I thank You that I am not like other people: swindlers, unjust, adulterers, or even like this tax collector. 'I fast twice a week; I pay tithes of all that I get.' "But the tax collector, standing some distance away, was even unwilling to lift up his eyes to heaven, but was beating his breast, saying, 'God, be merciful to me, the sinner!' "I tell you, this man went to his house justified rather than the other; for everyone who exalts himself will be humbled, but he who humbles himself will be exalted" (Luke. 18:10-14).

Our Western frame of reference is personal piety. This is about our individual lives of prayer. Jesus had more than personal piety in mind with this story. The two men went to pray in the temple courts before the Judge of all the earth and confess. Their prayers reflected two different hearts. They could have taken their concerns to their private prayer closets, but they came to the temple instead and stood together. God had promised to hear the confession of His people when they came into His courts as Solomon instructed. God was watching for and listening to the saints. The one with a Davidic heart was forgiven and went away justified. The other left unchanged and probably felt no need to return. David asked, "Who may ascend into the hill of the LORD? And who may stand in His holy place?" (Ps. 24:3). "He who has clean hands and a pure heart" (Ps. 24:4). The tax collector felt welcome to return. Jesus had more to say about watchfulness.

> Be on guard, so that your hearts will not be weighted down with dissipation and drunkenness and the worries of life, and that day will not come on you suddenly like a trap; for it will come upon all those who dwell on the face of all the earth. But keep on the alert at all times, praying that you may have strength to escape all these things that are about to take place, and to stand before the Son of Man. (Luke 21:34-36)

Isaiah provided a strategic view of the inner workings of God's house of prayer. "On your walls, O Jerusalem, I have appointed watchmen; All day and all night they will never keep silent. You who remind the LORD, take no rest for yourselves; And give Him no rest until He establishes And makes Jerusalem a praise in the earth" (Isa. 62:6-7). Our commanded posture is to be alert, guarding our hearts, aware of the times and seasons, and *praying at all times*. This will be especially true in the last of the last days but applies now as well. There is no place for casual, careless prayer, but the challenge for this praying at all times will be great. The worries of life war against prayer. As David noted, the House of Prayer is a place to gain strength (Ps. 68:35) and is a praying-at-all-times place.

Davidic worship attributes appear outside the gospels as well. After Jesus ascends into heaven, the 120 gather in the upper room for continual prayer (Acts 1:14). Fifty days later at Pentecost, the Spirit falls, Peter preaches, and 3,000 are added that day (Acts 2:41). The new converts were: "Day by day continuing with one mind in the temple, and breaking bread from house to house, they were taking their meals together with gladness and sincerity of heart" (Acts 2:46). They didn't need to be in the temple. Sacrifice was no longer needed, but being in the temple courts for prayer as Solomon directed was an invitation. Peter and John went up to the temple at the ninth hour, the hour of prayer (Acts 3:1). The healing they performed then so shocked those in the temple that the people ran to the apostles in Solomon's portico, inside the temple court, to hear how this miracle happened. David's marvelous deeds were at work (Ps. 65:5) as David said they would.

There was a late-night prayer meeting for Peter when he was thrown into prison. He later joined them to testify to his miraculous release. The early disciples were continually devoted to prayer. The apostles curtailed service to do more prayer and minister the word. Cornelius prayed constantly and gave alms to the poor. He was commended for his practice by an angel from heaven.

The writer to the Hebrews saw Jesus singing in the midst of the congregation (Heb. 2:12). It was a quote from David in Psalm 22:22. David was ministering to the congregation, singing God's praises. This would have very likely occurred in the House of Prayer, in the confines of David's tent and surrounding courts. Jesus was following David. The writer of Hebrews was not experiencing role confusion but expressing linkage between Jesus and David. It was a footprint. David is mentioned throughout the Bible, but most of the prophetic references point to Jesus—the greater David. David's greatest desire was for the House of Prayer. Jesus, like David, wanted to sing in the House of Prayer.

The House of Prayer was not active during Jesus's earthly ministry. Anna was a Davidic worshiper and welcomed Jesus to His house. Jesus, "who always lives to make intercession" (Heb. 7:25), was clearly troubled by the misuse of His Father's House of Prayer. He affirmed the *one thing* intimacy choice of Mary, approved night and day intercession for justice, and received the penitent publican's prayer in the temple courts as Solomon said He would. The early church was continually in prayer before Pentecost and after— albeit under the radar. As the gospel was preparing to go viral, the House of Prayer was at the helm—not in Jerusalem but in Antioch!

Chapter Sixteen

SHARATHING THE LORD AT ANTIOCH

Now there were at Antioch, in the church that was *there*, prophets and teachers: Barnabas, and Simeon who was called Niger, and Lucius of Cyrene, and Manaen who had been brought up with Herod the tetrarch, and Saul. While they were ministering to the Lord and fasting, the Holy Spirit said, Set apart for Me Barnabas and Saul for the work to which I have called them. (Acts 13:1-2)

The first missionary enterprise was the result of prayer and fasting (Acts 13:3). Luke, the presumed author of the book of Acts, chose his words carefully. The Greek word used in Acts 13:2, *minister*, and its lemma, or form, occurs ninety-six times in the Bible using the LXX *leitourgesai*. Only three of those occurrences are in the New Testament. It is a translation for the Hebrew *sharath*. Foreigners could now *sharath* the Lord (Isa. 56:6-7). The House of Prayer did not need the Ark, as Jeremiah intimated (Jer. 3:16), nor the tent and artifacts to operate. It didn't need Aaron. It didn't need Levi. It didn't need the temple. It didn't even need Jerusalem or Israel—Antioch was in Syria. The House of Prayer was portable, as seen by Malachi. It just needed a location, which God provided, and a 24/7 Davidic heart and worship. Converted Greeks (Gentiles) provided some of this Davidic passion, as Isaiah foretold. Luke doesn't tell us if the Antioch folks followed a night and day schedule, but the use of *leitourgesai* suggests they understood Davidic worship. The sharath of the Lord—the sacrificial service *to* the Master from a forgiven, cleansed, humble, faithful and intimate heart that generates the remarkable, delightful and deeply satisfying experience *of* the Master—went on in the early church. A new chapter for a missions mandate to reach the nations with awesome deeds, even to the ends of the earth and the farthest sea, had opened as David had foreseen (Psalm 65:1-5).

When Paul and Barnabas stopped in, they received their commission to the nations. God chose this event to push the next chapter of the great commission. The Sovereign God quite naturally spoke out of the atmosphere of *sharath*ing. The great commission follows the great devotion!

In addition to Jerusalem, God had now chosen Antioch to disclose His will in the context of a *sharath*ing people. He was informing the church, just as He had done in Moses' tent when the people learned God's will concerning the new challenge: the inheritance rights of the daughters of Zelophehad (Num. 27:7). God's new plan? It was time for a missions outreach trip.

Jerusalem would be the ultimate place of God's choosing, but there would be other places where God would disclose His will in the context of a *sharath*ing, testifying people. The disciples would be sent out to give testimony even to the remotest parts of the earth: "but you will receive power when the Holy Spirit has come upon you; and you shall be My witnesses both in Jerusalem, and in all Judea and Samaria, and even to the remotest part of the earth" (Acts 1:8). Malachi was correct. There would be global incense locations (Mal. 1:11) and testimony. Foreigners, graciously brought near, would *sharath* the Lord, not only in Jerusalem, but abroad.

There are two other instances of *leitourgesai* in the New Testament. One is found in the book of Hebrews and is a reference to a priest ministering to the Lord through temple sacrifice (Heb. 10:11). This is an expected usage of the word. The other New Testament usage occurs in the book of Romans. Paul reminded the Gentile saints of their indebtedness to Jews. They needed to *minister* to the Jews materially (Rom. 15:27). This too was an appropriate charge to the Gentile church and will be discussed later in the chapter on Israel.

*Sharath*ing or ministering to the Lord is central in the Old Testament. It seems strange that only three references to its Septuagint Greek word *leitourgesai* are found in the New Testament. According to the *Theological Dictionary of the New Testament* (TDNT), a more commonly used term in the New Testament is *latreuo* (Friedrich 1971, Volume 4, 61). TDNT found *latreuein* to be religious service or conduct in general rather than *leitourgein*, which includes Aaronic priestly functions. Paul provides an important linkage between the two word groups.

> who are Israelites, to whom belongs the
> adoption as sons, and the glory and the cov-
> enants and the giving of the Law and the
> *temple* service and the promises, whose are
> the fathers, and from whom is the Christ
> according to the flesh, who is over all, God
> blessed forever. Amen. (Rom. 9:4-5)

Paul listed out the astounding contribution of Jews. The most significant contribution was Jesus, but Paul mentioned the *temple service*. However, Paul used the Greek word *latreia* (noun, verb *latreuo*). Temple is provided by the translator to orient the reader. Why Paul chose to use *latreuo* over the obvious *leitourgesai* is not apparent, but the context is clear. It may have been important to move away from the liturgical understanding of *sharath* to accommodate the move away from the more narrowly defined temple service. *Latreuo* accommodates and in some instances implies *sharath* elements.

Anna, who had several Davidic worship characteristics, was said to *latreuo* the Lord. Matthew used this same term to describe Jesus's response to Satan in the three temptation trials: "Then Jesus said to him, Go, Satan! For it is written, 'YOU SHALL WORSHIP THE LORD YOUR GOD, AND SERVE HIM ONLY'" (Matt. 4:10). Only God was to be worshiped (*latreuo*) and Jesus wanted His Father to be deeply satisfied by His service. It was a family affair.

Similarly Paul told the Romans about acceptable *latreuo* (service). "Therefore I urge you, brethren, by the mercies of God, to present your bodies a living and holy sacrifice, acceptable to God, *which* is your spiritual service of worship"

(Rom. 12:1). God was after living sacrifices. As David might have described, it was the vertically oriented sacrifice of praise and thanksgiving, a First Commandment devoted heart, and 24/7 intercessory worship and practice. It was his burden to have a resting place for the mighty one of Jacob and a zeal for His house. This was acceptable worship in its full context.

In his defense before King Agrippa, Paul provided this concluding remark: "*the promise* to which our twelve tribes hope to attain, as they earnestly serve *God* night and day. And for this hope, O King, I am being accused by Jews" (Acts 26:7). Night and day is Davidic language. The House of Prayer and service went on 24/7. It wasn't casual service as Rehoboam might have supplied, but with earnest perseverance as David had done.

Two more New Testament accounts are understood better from a Davidic worship context. Paul and Silas were thrown into the Philippian jail. "But about midnight Paul and Silas were praying and singing hymns of praise to God, and the prisoners were listening to them" (Acts 16:25). It was not a time for sleep. It wasn't a preaching moment. It was a time to draw men through Davidic worship or intercessory worship. They prayed and sang. The night watch was at work again. The prisoners listened. The House of Prayer mission was functioning. God's power—His awesome deeds—was released. Once the doors were flung open and the jailer was about to commit suicide, Paul and Silas were able to intervene and teach the way and get folks saved. The order of events is noteworthy.

Paul wrote to the Thessalonians, "Rejoice always; pray without ceasing; in everything give thanks; for this is God's will for you in Christ Jesus" (1 Thess. 5:16-18). Rejoicing, incessant praying, and thanksgiving. These must be understood within the context of scriptures and not simply something we understand through today's lens. Without an Old Testament context for Davidic worship and intercession, it is easy to see this as a simple encouragement. It may be a simple command to be wholehearted and have an attitude of prayer. This is certainly a worthy goal. However, given the Old Testament example of David and Paul's extensive training and understanding of the OT, it may be better to view this as a command to a growing citywide (Thessaloniki) church to pursue a House of Prayer practice—Davidic worship. Organize yourselves to build First Commandment devotion, give thanks, rejoice, pray, and sing 24/7 — without ceasing. It will draw men just as David foresaw.

One is tempted to ask, "If *sharath*ing was a bedrock to evangelism and worship, why did it not take off and dominate the church landscape when it could?" As the New Testament testifies, the House of Prayer was not dominant, even after persecution lessened in the fourth century under Constantine, when it seemed that the last of the major obstacles to the House of Prayer had been removed. Luke provided a critical answer to this question.

Chapter Seventeen

The Jerusalem Council

The Jerusalem council of Acts 15 provides a key perspective on the delay of the restoration of the House of Prayer. Shortly before His death, Jesus spoke about the coming destruction of the temple and the disciples asked, "Tell us, when will these things happen, and what *will be* the sign of Your coming, and of the end of the age? (Matt. 24:3)." Jesus didn't answer them directly but warned them about being misled as to the timing of His return. And in Acts 1:6, after the resurrection, the disciples asked the question again. "Lord, is it at this time You are restoring the kingdom to Israel?" (Acts 1:6). Once more, Jesus redirected the conversation. The disciples would not be privy to the times and seasons the Father had set. The hope for a quick return of Christ was there, and the very questions they asked suggested an expectation that it would be sooner rather than later. Amos 9:11 must be just around the corner. Jesus could have given a blunt answer to the question, but chose not to.

The immediate question before the council was what to do with Gentiles streaming to Christ. Was this Psalm 65:5 that David saw? The Pharisees in the group believed the Gentiles should follow Moses (Acts 15:5). In the end, the council concluded that Gentiles should not be burdened by Moses, and a letter to this effect was sent to the churches through the hand of Paul and Barnabas. James justified this approach based on an Old Testament quote (Amos 9:11), and the apostles, elders and the church, who had gathered, agreed. Why he used this verse seems curious at first. He turned to a passage about David.

James, like the apostles, believed the Lord's return was close at hand. James told the brethren the Gentile mission grew out of God's promise to restore the fallen tabernacle (Amos 9:11 *booth,* Hebrew *sukkah*) of David. The book of Acts was written around AD 63. Nero was the emperor—a truly wicked despot and a great candidate for the man of lawlessness. Israel was a nation. The temple was still standing. The greater David—Jesus—was coming back very soon to consummate the kingdom. Davidic intercessory-like worship was occurring among Jews and Greeks in the early church (Acts 2; 10; 12; 13; 16), albeit under the radar because of persecution. Jews were turning to Christ in Israel and now among the Gentiles, with great missional impact. Paul was clear when he wrote to the Galatians that God would justify the Gentiles and fulfill His promise to Abraham (Gal. 3:8). James saw the end of the age was in sight for the early church. Amos 9:11-13, an eschatological passage, was going to be fulfilled before their eyes. The room must have been charged with expectation.

> 'AFTER THESE THINGS I will return, AND
> I WILL REBUILD THE TABERNACLE
> OF DAVID WHICH HAS FALLEN, AND
> I WILL REBUILD ITS RUINS, AND

I WILL RESTORE IT, SO THAT THE
REST OF MANKIND MAY SEEK THE
LORD, AND ALL THE GENTILES WHO
ARE CALLED BY MY NAME,' SAYS
THE LORD, WHO MAKES THESE
THINGS KNOWN FROM LONG AGO.
(Acts 15:16-18)

James used the term *tabernacle* or *tent* in his reporting, Greek *skene*. This term was used by the Hebrew Septuagint translators as well as the New Testament writers. James quoted a portion of the Amos passage in Acts 15:16-17, but changed the flavor in verse 17. If he was using an Old Testament variant for his quote, it is unknown to us. In contrast to Amos, James recorded "THAT THE REST OF MANKIND MAY SEEK THE LORD, AND ALL THE GENTILES WHO ARE CALLED BY MY NAME" (Acts 15:17). He heard Paul and Barnabas's account and saw a great harvest of souls coming from among the Gentiles; he undoubtedly made the connection to Abraham's promise as Paul had.

The term for *seek* that Luke chose is used in Hebrews 11:6. God is a rewarder of those who believe and diligently seek after Him (KJV). It is a careful search (1 Pet. 1:10). It is thorough and complete (Luke 11:50-51), a heartfelt searching (Heb. 12:17) although used negatively with Esau. This heartfelt, diligent seeking is in line with how David's tent operated. God, the one who answers prayer, would draw all flesh (Ps. 65:2-4) to come and dwell in His courts (intimacy). It stands in contrast to Amos's militant tone as he considered Edom and the nations.

God described Himself as moving about in a tent into the time of David. "For I have not dwelt in a house since the day I brought up the sons of Israel from Egypt, even to this day; but I have been moving about in a tent, even in a tabernacle" (2 Sam. 7:6). God had been moving about in a Hebrew *ohel* (tent) that became a *mishkan* (sanctuary) when His Ark was placed there. The Septuagint Greek for the same passage had God moving about in a *katalumati* or guest house that became a *skene*. When David set up his *ohel* for the Ark, the Septuagint called it a *skene* (2 Sam. 6:17).

In the TDNT, we find *skene* occurs 435 times in the LXX; sixty-five times, there is no corresponding Hebrew text; 245 times, it is the translation of *ohel*; ninety-three times, it is the translation for *mishkan*; and twenty-five times for *succoth/sukkah* and variations (Friedrich 1971, Volume 7, 369) and seven other miscellaneous uses. *Skene* is used to translate the three major Hebrew terms: *ohel*, *mishkan*, and *succoth*. *Skene* is broader than we think and can legitimately refer to David's tent (*ohel*) experience.

It appears Luke added a Holy Spirit-inspired understanding in verse 17; therefore, it is appropriate to see *skene* as a composite term covering all three Hebrew words and their corresponding usages. Restoration, as Luke saw it, would be reconciling—drawing in lost souls as David's House of Prayer would understand, fulfilling Abraham's blessing. Houses of Prayer around the world would have the simplicity of David's tent. Believers would *sharath* the Lord 24/7 with instrumentally assisted declarations, prayers and songs of praise from forgiven and intimate hearts. These House of Prayer offerings would result in the deeply satisfying experience *of* the Master. This partnering with the

Master in His house would drive a missions outreach to the nations, drawing all men from the ends of the earth with awesome and marvelous deeds to come dwell in His courts. It would cry out for God's purposes for Israel — making "Jerusalem a praise in all the earth" (Isa. 62:7) — a place of worship, a place of salvation, provision, enjoyment and much more. The House of Prayer would cry out for God's purposes for the nations, declaring to Abraham "And in you all the families of the earth will be blessed" (Gen. 12:3).

Houses of Prayer would be a sanctuary to encounter the face of God in intimacy and gladness of heart. The missional approach to the final harvest would have a great deal to do with David rather than Moses, as Luke noted. Restoration would eventually be governmental, as Amos had seen, with the greater David returning and ruling His Kingdom with the rod of iron (Ps. 2:9). But the restoration would start with the hand of mercy. It would start with the House of Prayer and an invitation to intimacy, walking and partnering with God (dwelling in His courts, Ps. 65:4).

Although the missionary success of Paul and Barnabas was stellar, history shows that the full measure of the restored tabernacle of David was yet future. Jesus, the Davidic king, did not return as the apostles expected. The temple was later destroyed, and Israel was expelled from the land. The promise for the House of Prayer, a restoration of faithful Israel and a great harvest that Luke saw, was for another time. It will eclipse what even Paul and Barnabas had experienced. Most likely, it will eclipse every revival that has been released in the earth. It will be an unparalleled, dramatic harvest fit for the coming King.

As noted in the previous chapter, God showed the House of Prayer did not require the tent of meeting, the Ark of the Covenant, a temple, Jerusalem, Levitical workers, Aaronic priests, or any specific location (the Spirit had been poured out, and many locations were now possible). There were foreigners ready to man the walls of intercession, providing night and day Davidic worship.

The House of Prayer would be a sign of the impending end of the age as well as a provision for that time. But the mission and full release of the House of Prayer was also tied to the recovery of Israel, as seen by both Amos and Luke, and there was a long wait for that. Israel was forgotten until 1948. God's promises connected to Israel and the land He gave them began to stir again. Chapter Eighteen takes a deeper look at the Israel and the Church.

Since the House of Prayer will be recovered in the last days, Chapter Nineteen will explore the expectations for that season.

THE ISRAEL CONNECTION

Israel is significant to the restoration of the House of Prayer, and the House of Prayer is significant to the restoration of Israel. This is God's intention. For over 2,000 years, there was no Israel. Early persecution of the church came at the hands of the Jews, but soon enough, the shoe was on the other foot. It is fair to say that church persecution of Jews, directly or indirectly, through word and deed, was overwhelmingly more brutal, widespread, and longer lasting. Judaism was vilified in the eyes of the church. As a result, it was not too difficult to eventually embrace the view of replacement theology: Since Israel was faithless, all the promises should now be applied to the faithful church. Ironically, the church today looks very much like faithless Israel. The proverbial pot calling the kettle black. The promises to Israel were greatly spiritualized to accomplish this misdirection.

Since Israel was replaced by the church, according to replacement theology, the Old Testament as a whole became suspect as well: it was now thought largely irrelevant. The New Testament was now the real mission. Important Old Testament revelatory information was lost in this perspective, the House of Prayer being one of the casualties. It died with Israel and the temple. In addition to lost revelation, the last days events, deeply rooted in the Old Testament, also became obscure. This helped saints disengage further from the Old Testament, and an "it will all pan out in the end" view of the last days arose. More on this topic will be addressed in the following chapter.

Replacement theology is scandalous and has helped support terrible evil, both in practice and theology. The apostle Paul provided the correct perspective. "For I am not ashamed of the gospel, for it is the power of God for salvation to everyone who believes, to the Jew first and also to the Greek" (Rom. 1:16). Salvation through Jesus is available to all. The gospel is the good news, but it does not stand on its own. It points beyond the label. It is the gospel of the kingdom. Jesus, David's heir, and His kingdom are the good news, and the content of the gospel is defined in this context.

There is only one name that is given to men by which they may be saved (Acts 4:12). This is true for everyone. There are no exceptions prospectively or retrospectively. Everyone in heaven will have accepted the Bridegroom God and His Son. Paul is not trying to point out the obvious, but rather the linkage between Jews and Gentiles and God's priority. They have a shared destiny and, in many ways, a shared experience and path.

> If the first piece *of dough* is holy, the lump is also; and if the root is holy, the branches are too. But if some of the branches were broken off, and you, being a wild olive, were grafted in among them and became

partaker with them of the rich root of the olive tree, do not be arrogant toward the branches; but if you are arrogant, *remember that* it is not you who supports the root, but the root supports you. You will say then, Branches were broken off so that I might be grafted in. Quite right, they were broken off for their unbelief, but you stand by your faith. Do not be conceited, but fear; for if God did not spare the natural branches, He will not spare you, either. (Rom. 11:16-21)

Paul told the Gentile believers—the wild olive branch—to learn from the natural olive branch. Both groups have a common root. Both are subject to the root. Gentiles have been grafted into the vine and stay in that place because of faith. Conceit is an ever-present temptation. Unbelief is only a step away. Any branch can be broken off if needed. The Gentiles partook with them—Jewish believers in Jesus—and did not originate God's plan of salvation as some might believe or practice. Abraham, David and the prophets and other Israelites laid the foundation for salvation.

Over time, the flavor of the church became increasingly Gentile. When Jews got saved, which became rare, they joined the church. However, unbelieving Jews are simply coming home when they trust in Jesus. They may end up in any number of denominations, independent churches, or messianic synagogues. It is a choice, as it is for all believers, but they are coming home to an existing spiritual kingdom established long ago.

Israel is God's firstborn son. "Then you shall say to Pharaoh, 'Thus says the LORD, Israel is My son, My first-born'" (Ex. 4:22). The Bridegroom God has a family order. In the ancient world, more honor was given to the firstborn, and more was required of the firstborn as well. God will deal with Israel as a firstborn errant son, whether they like the idea or not. They will receive either the discipline of their heavenly Father or the judgment of their Father. The younger brother in the adoptive family should pay close attention.

Although Isaiah was told to render Israel deaf and blind (Isa. 6:10), God was not done with her. "Go and proclaim these words toward the north and say, 'Return, faithless Israel,' declares the LORD; 'I will not look upon you in anger. For I am gracious,' declares the LORD; 'I will not be angry forever'" (Jer. 3:12). God would be faithful even though Israel was faithless. God's anger toward Israel will not last forever. What He promises, He delivers. "From the standpoint of the gospel they are enemies for your sake, but from the standpoint of God's choice they are beloved for the sake of the fathers; for the gifts and the calling of God are irrevocable" (Rom. 11:28-29).

He will recover Israel. He has not set Israel aside without remedy. His calling is irrevocable. He will not change requirements, lower the bar to accomplish His work, nor transfer His calling to another. "But *it is* not as though the word of God has failed. For they are not all Israel who are *descended* from Israel" (Rom. 9:6). The word *descended* was added by the translators. The KJV is better: not all Israel is Israel.

Because it is a family affair, God will deal with the church in a similar way to how He will deal with Israel. Not all the church is the church. Israel always had a mix of belief and unbelief, and so does the church. There will be a refined nation of Israel (believers in Yeshua) and a pure church from which one new man will be created (Eph. 2:15). The work of the cross has been completed, but the final phase of the new man is still future.

> I say then, they did not stumble so as to fall, did they? May it never be! But by their transgression salvation *has come* to the Gentiles, to make them jealous. Now if their transgression is riches for the world and their failure is riches for the Gentiles, how much more will their fulfillment be! (Rom. 11:11-12)

The temporary disobedience of Israel brought salvation to the Gentiles, which is the baseline of Paul's comparison. There is a *much more* coming when Israel obeys. God is planning a multiplier of amazing experience in the last days—the how *much more* (Rom. 11:15). The dawn is rising. In a casual conversation with a missionary from Israel, he reported that in the early 1980s, there were perhaps two dozen messianic fellowships. By 2013 there were now over 260 messianic fellowships, and the number was rising steadily. The numbers were estimates, but the magnitude of change was clear. God is saving Israel. And of course, this increase continues to occur as the House of Prayer locations around the world also increase.

David's House of Prayer intercession was commanded. Intercession for Jerusalem went up in the tent, and God promised to supply watchmen (Isa. 62:6-7). It would be the foreigners crying out to Him who would make the difference.

> I will pour out on the house of David and
> on the inhabitants of Jerusalem, the Spirit of
> grace and of supplication, so that they will
> look on Me whom they have pierced; and
> they will mourn for Him, as one mourns for
> an only son, and they will weep bitterly over
> Him like the bitter weeping over a firstborn.
> (Zech. 12:10)

The intercession of Isaiah 62 watchmen will eventually cause the removal of the blinders and earplugs from Israel. It will be a sad time for a short season, as all the pieces of Israel's history fall into place, and Israel recognizes the enormity of what has transpired. This will happen in the last days, but in the last of the last days, there will be a surge of recognition. Those destined to salvation will receive grace and the ability to intercede. They will take their rightful place on Isaiah's wall with God's foreigners. A praying Israel will have a stunning impact on the world. Neither the older nor the younger brother will have a reason to boast. Disdain for each other will be completely removed.

At some point, all Israel will be saved (Rom. 11:26). The events that will surface to accomplish this are still unclear, but as more of the last days puzzle pieces fall into place, the clarity goes up.

In Romans 11:12, Paul set the bar of expectation. Israel's failure led to the salvation of Gentiles. For the past 2,000-plus years, the Gentile harvest has come in and in great numbers through various revivals down through the church age. Paul tells the church in Rome that Israel's reconciliation will have *much more* impact in the world than Israel's failure produced. When all Israel is saved—the surviving portion Zechariah saw—something even more amazing will happen to bless the Gentile church that has been fervently praying for and standing with Israel. Paul looked into the future at the multiplier effect of a believing Israel and made this comment: "For if their rejection is the reconciliation of the world, what will *their* acceptance be but life from the dead?" (Rom. 11:15). It will be a *much more*—a multiplier of blessing. Israel will be a blessing in all the earth as promised (Gen. 12:2-3). God's promise to Abraham will not fail.

Foreign watchman will cry out (Isa. 56, 57)—a role the saints today are fulfilling. The church will also be awakened (Eph. 5:14). Intimacy will be rediscovered (Isa. 62:4-5), which will propel and sustain increasing First Commandment *sharath*ing in an awakened church. Israel will see Jesus and get saved. Great turmoil will be going on at the same time (Joel 2:11). Israel will experience significant losses (Zech. 13:8). The church will struggle with apostasy (2 Thess. 2:3-4) but get cleaned up. Revival and prayer will hit high gear (Rev. 5:8) and renewed power in the gospel of the King will surge (Rom. 11:11-12). There will be a great harvest (Acts 15:17), martyrs, men and women with sterling testimonies, awesome deeds and then judgment will follow the King's return (Isa. 63:1-4). It will be the world's darkest hour and the saints' finest hour. God has a very close relationship planned for His family.

> For Macedonia and Achaia have been pleased to make a contribution for the poor among the saints in Jerusalem. Yes, they were pleased to do so, and they are indebted to them. For if the Gentiles have shared in their spiritual things, they are indebted to minister to them also in material things. (Rom. 15:26-27)

Paul took up a collection for the saints in Jerusalem. It was used to help the poor. But he attached the significance of this action to *sharath*ing – the voluntary service with love. *Sharath*ing would be applied not only to God, as evidenced in the House of Prayer activity, but also more broadly with Jewish saints and Jews who may or may not be saints. Paul described this *sharath*ing satisfaction as provoking the Jews to jealousy (Rom. 11:14). Given the church's notorious treatment of Jews throughout history, the notion that the church will *sharath* the Jews with pleasurable service will create utter astonishment among Jews.

They will need material help as well as the prayer that rises from the House of Prayer. They will need their brother to stand up to any bullying that comes their way. This was true in Paul's day, but the opportunity to help and identify with family members will come again, especially in the last days—the time of Jacob's trouble.

A quick look at the last days and Israel's part in them is necessary at this point.

Chapter Nineteen

THE LAST DAYS

The restoration of the House of Prayer is tied to Israel, and also tied to the last days (Acts 15:16-17). Some general comments on the last days are appropriate. When it comes to considering the last days, believers have very mixed opinions and emotions. This chapter was added because of God's concern for Israel and our support of Israel in prayer and resources. It is also for those who feel confused by the whole thing, have thrown up their hands and in frustration declared, "It will all work out in the end."

While one can appreciate the frustration, an outcome that simply works out in the end may not at all be what one expects or has prepared for. And this may prove to be disastrous for some. A great deal has been written on the last days, and this will not be a systematic study. Rather, it is intended to provide a framework to help in the study of night and day prayer.

The last days are like a puzzle. Certainly, Adam knew Satan would lose in the end, but he had very little detail beyond what God had given at that point. Over time, God has revealed more facets. The Bridegroom God has served up some of the detail with a measure of uncertainty. It lacks the full clarity we desire. There are plenty of loose ends, and faith is required.

As with Moses' tent and David's tent, God uses the entire Bible as a filter. He knows our hearts when we often do not. The filtering is just enough to expose our hearts. Will adversity, delay, or uncertainty turn us away in frustration? Are we really bride material? Will we turn away if not everything is explained in our desired timeframe and to our satisfaction? Or worse, will we simply ignore it and float down the river of time?

Jesus prayed, "I praise Thee, O Father, Lord of heaven and earth, that Thou didst hide these things from the wise and intelligent and didst reveal them to babes" (Luke 10:21). The problem is the heart, not the mind. A corrupt heart will corrupt the whole man, whether he is bright or simple. The intelligent have a greater risk of corruption and must watch over their hearts with greater care. Godly wisdom that manages intellect has immense value (Prov. 1:5).

God told Aaron and Miriam He spoke in dark sayings (Num. 12:8). Jesus told His disciples this manner of revelation would continue. He, too, spoke in parables or dark sayings (Matt. 13:35, quoting from Ps.78:2) and even His disciples weren't always given the interpretation. This is normal Christianity. He hasn't changed and won't. True insight is not necessarily given to bright saints, but to child-like ones! Insight is given to those who ask, seek, and knock (Matt. 7:7), and to those who continue to seek and press in (Mark 4:25). The fear of the Lord is the beginning of wisdom (Prov. 1:7). Humility comes before honor (1 Pet. 5:5-7) and most likely before true insight. A measure of continuing mystery is intentional. It provokes our search (Prov. 25:2). He loves the Berean saint.

Peter learned a difficult lesson. Jesus told His disciples to eat His body and drink His blood. Regardless of one's theology, these are very strange words.

> Therefore many of His disciples, when they heard *this* said, "This is a difficult statement; who can listen to it?" But Jesus, conscious that His disciples grumbled at this, said to them, "Does this cause you to stumble? ... As a result of this many of His disciples withdrew and were not walking with Him anymore. So Jesus said to the twelve, "You do not want to go away also, do you?" Simon Peter answered Him, "Lord, to whom shall we go? You have words of eternal life." (John 6:60-61, 66-68)

Jesus actively confronted His disciples. Would they trust their own rational instincts over his words? Peter actively chose to orient his life around Jesus's words and not his own. What we know of the universe will always be incomplete, and we must submit to the words of Jesus. This notion offends us. We want the final appeal on matters of life and death and right and wrong to be our own. We want to be able to justify ourselves. This is not Jesus's way. He will always say, "Come to Me" (Matt. 11:28).

> Then the kingdom of heaven will be comparable to ten virgins, who took their lamps

and went out to meet the bridegroom. "Five
of them were foolish, and five were prudent.
"For when the foolish took their lamps, they
took no oil with them, but the prudent took
oil in flasks along with their lamps. "Now
while the bridegroom was delaying, they
all got drowsy and *began* to sleep. "But
at midnight there was a shout, 'Behold,
the bridegroom! Come out to meet *him*'.
(Matt. 25:1-6)

Jesus tells the parable of the wedding to address the issue
of watchfulness and preparedness of His Bride. Perhaps
the five foolish virgins had interpreted the delay of the
Bridegroom as an opportunity to pursue other activities and
distractions. They incorrectly believed that they would have
enough time later to get ready. When the Bridegroom did
arrive, there was no longer any time to get ready. They were
unable to follow Him into the wedding feast. The door was
shut. This is a sobering warning for the church. We are called
to vigilant watchfulness. When the appointed time comes for
the return of our King, we must be ready to immediately rise
up and follow Him. Again, the wise believer will study the
Scriptures for understanding of all these things.

Jesus told His disciples to be alert, praying at all times
(Luke 21:36). He corrected the Pharisees.

The Pharisees and Sadducees came up,
and testing Jesus, they asked Him to show
them a sign from heaven. But He replied to
them, "When it is evening, you say, '*It will*

be fair weather, for the sky is red.' "And in
the morning, '*There will be* a storm today,
for the sky is red and threatening.' Do you
know how to discern the appearance of the
sky, but cannot *discern* the signs of the
times? (Matt. 16:1-3)

They should have been watching for the signs of the
times. Part of being alert is fulfilling your assignment (Matt.
24:45-47), and part of it is watching for the Master's return.
It would be nice to argue that fulfilling your assignment is
all that God requires. This notion is incorrect. The signs of
the times matter, but only have value to the watcher.

"But of that day or hour no one knows, not even the angels
in heaven, nor the Son, but the Father *alone*. 'Take heed,
keep on the alert; for you do not know when the *appointed*
time will come'" (Mark 13:32-33). Jesus's instructions feel
contradictory. Why would one watch for the signs of the
times when the hour and day are unknown? The day and
the hour of Christ's return are truly unknown today. They
are, however, part of a sequence of time-related events or
countdown that has not been released by the Father. Once
the countdown sequence is initiated by the Father, there is a
great deal of information on the timetable of Christ's return
and the timing of future actions.

Paul warned his new Thessalonian church about the last
days. His letter to them may have come within several weeks
of his evangelizing mission there.

Let no one in any way deceive you, for *it
will not come* unless the apostasy comes

> first, and the man of lawlessness is revealed,
> the son of destruction, who opposes and
> exalts himself above every so-called god or
> object of worship, so that he takes his seat
> in the temple of God, displaying himself as
> being God. (2 Thess. 2:3-4)

This very unsavory person was described as a son of destruction and actually displayed himself as God in the temple. This deceptive leader must be revealed before Jesus returns. It is one of many signs of the times to help alert and orient the saints.

Daniel provides intriguing information on time periods. He speaks of a seven-year period, literally a week of years. A leader will come and establish and then break his agreement or covenant with Israel. This event doesn't appear to have taken place yet, from what we know of history. It appears to be future.

> And he will make a firm covenant with the
> many for one week but in the middle of
> the week he will put a stop to sacrifice and
> grain offering; and on the wing of abomi-
> nations will come one who makes desolate,
> even until a complete destruction, one that
> is decreed, is poured out on the one who
> makes desolate. (Dan. 9:27)

Someone is coming who will put an end to Jewish sacrifice and cause desolation for forty-two months (or three-and-a-half years or 1,260 days) after making an initial covenant.

At the beginning of the twentieth century, this seemed most unlikely. There was no Israel, no temple, and no unsavory leader making agreements with them. Watching is important. One domino is in place. Israel is a nation again, not a righteous nation as God calls righteous, but a nation nonetheless.

In his revelation, John speaks of a tyrannical leader who is coming. He further identifies him in Revelation 12:9. In his vision, he saw Satan, represented by a great dragon, in league with a terrible leader represented by a beast.

> There was given to him [beast] a mouth
> speaking arrogant words and blasphemies,
> and authority to act for forty-two months
> was given to him. And he opened his mouth
> in blasphemies against God, to blaspheme
> His name and His tabernacle, *that is,* those
> who dwell in heaven. It was also given to
> him to make war with the saints and to over-
> come them, and authority over every tribe
> and people and tongue and nation was given
> to him. (Rev. 13:5-7)

Daniel, Paul, and John did not synchronize their accounts to provide a rock-solid connection, but they knew God was going to do something around Israel. A seven-year period is coming. A truly evil person will arise and delude Israel into making an agreement with him rather than trusting God. That evil leader will break his agreement halfway through the seven-year period and open a reign of terror that will last exactly forty-two months. Just before the marriage supper of the Lamb, Jesus will return with His army (Rev. 19:19-21) and destroy this leader and his supporters, ushering in His dominion. The countdown for this has not yet been released by the Father, so the hour and day remain unknown—for now. But all can watch for the season.

God has last days instructions about coming events, actions He is taking, and actions we should take. If His children aren't watching, they will not be able to pick up the gamers' *key* and play successfully. The House of Prayer is a last days key! Miss the key and the game is much harder to play.

There will be a second coming of Christ. There is certainly debate around the details, but Christians know Jesus is returning. Six general statements should be highlighted surrounding His return and the end of the age events.

First, if your view either doesn't allow for Israel at all or sends Israel down a completely independent path, you should be suspicious. The gospel and storylines for Jews and Gentiles are inseparably linked. "To the Jew first and also to the Gentile" (Rom. 1:16). It is a family affair, and the family will cross the line together. God will reconcile His family.

John's book of Revelation has a grand mix of clear speech, metaphors, symbols and allegory. Readers of John's Revelation should start with words as clear speech and only move to other figures of speech when the context calls for it. They must realize that as they leave behind clear speech, clarity goes down, and the risk for misunderstanding and misapplication goes up. John saw the coming cosmic last days events. His comments are helpful. We are given a window into the relationship of the church and Israel.

> A great sign appeared in heaven: a woman clothed with the sun, and the moon under her feet, and on her head a crown of twelve stars; and she was with child; and she cried out, being in labor and in pain to give birth. Then another sign appeared in heaven: and behold, a great red dragon having seven heads and ten horns, and on his heads *were* seven diadems. And his tail swept away a third of the stars of heaven and threw them to the earth. And the dragon stood before the woman who was about to give birth, so that when she gave birth he might devour her child. And she gave birth to a son, a male *child*, who is to rule all the nations with a rod of iron; and her child was caught up to God and to His throne. Then the woman fled into the wilderness where she had a place prepared by God, so that there she would be nourished for one thousand two hundred and sixty days. (Rev. 12:1-6)

The Bridegroom God had this account recorded this way on purpose. He wants to draw the bride—not trick, deceive, or confuse her. The enemy of our souls has that assignment. We need to look deeper.

John sees a male child in Revelation 12:5. It is a male child and should be taken at face value. This portion is clear speech. The male child is caught up to the throne of God. He will rule the nations. Since John often alludes to the Old Testament, understanding who this might be is somewhat straightforward. John quoted from Psalm 2, a messianic Psalm. The male child who was caught up to God and rules with a rod of iron was the greater David, the Messiah, Jesus.

Knowing Jesus is involved makes the rest of this section easier to understand. Each piece of the puzzle that is solved makes subsequent pieces easier to solve. The woman who bore Jesus takes more work. Jesus's mother was Mary. In John's account, the woman who bore Jesus escapes to the wilderness where she stays for 1,260 days, or forty-two months. Notice that the time framework is the same as Daniel's. There is no record that the historical Mary ever needed to do this, so the woman is probably symbolic.

Mary was, of course, Jewish, and may represent Israel who gave us the Messiah. This is further confirmed in verse one of this chapter. John is again alluding to an Old Testament story. Joseph had a dream. He saw the sun, the moon, and eleven stars bowing down to him. It was a reference to his mom and dad and eleven other brothers. His father Jacob, who had been given the name Israel, understood the dream referred to Israel's family and sons (Gen. 37:9). Israel had twelve sons, and his descendants became the nation of Israel. It is very likely the woman in this passage represents Israel who gave us the messiah.

> And when the dragon saw that he was thrown down to the earth, he persecuted the woman who gave birth to the male child. But the two wings of the great eagle were given to the woman, so that she could fly into the wilderness to her place, where she was nourished for a time and times and half

a time, from the presence of the serpent.
(Rev. 12:13-14).

There is no historical record of Israel's descendants being protected for forty-two months (time and times and half a time). It must be a yet future event. The persecution of Jews in these last days is clear. "So the dragon was enraged with the woman, and went off to make war with the rest of her children, who keep the commandments of God and hold to the testimony of Jesus" (Rev. 12:17). Satan hates those who love Jesus and are linked to the woman. Those who love Jesus and obey Him—Christians—are the offspring of the woman. It is again, a family affair, whether they are natural or wild branches; they too will experience persecution in this coming period.

Suggesting that one member of the family will not willingly be present to help the other in their hour of greatest need would be odd indeed. One of the distinguishing characteristics of the last days will be the family support for both the natural and wild branches. It is obvious the wild branch (gentile church) will need to stand with the natural branch in their hour of trouble and discipline. Any theology that eliminates, replaces, spiritualizes, or marginalizes Israel should be suspect. John recorded Satan's vengeful actions, and this should be warning to the entire family of God. Satan is coming after the woman and her offspring!

Second, if your last days view is completely worked out, beware. "He said, 'Go *your way*, Daniel, for *these* words are concealed and sealed up until the end time'" (Dan. 12:9). God told Daniel to seal up parts of the revelation he was given until the time of the end. So the greater clarity will not come until that timeframe. They may well be hidden in plain sight. There is no way to know if what we don't know is material to our understanding until what is hidden has been released. "When the seven peals of thunder had spoken, I was about to write; and I heard a voice from heaven saying, 'Seal up the things which the seven peals of thunder have spoken and do not write them'" (Rev. 10:4). John noted that some details aren't revealed at any time. We just know there is more detail but don't know the content. Humility will help minimize this risk of needing to have it all worked out.

Third, if your philosophy on the last days pushes the return of Christ into the distant future, you should be concerned. Events that are way in the future, or aren't tied to anything in particular, often are forgotten or neglected. They become a litmus test of faith only and have little or no bearing on how we live today or what we should expect tomorrow. "Jesus is coming back" is a reassuring statement. But Jesus's return tied to knowable events rapidly coming upon us has much greater urgency.

> "Who then is the faithful and sensible slave whom his master put in charge of his household to give them their food at the proper time? Blessed is that slave whom his master finds so doing when he comes. Truly I say to you that he will put him in charge of all his possessions. But if that evil slave says in his heart, 'My master is not coming for a long time.'" (Matt. 24:45-48)

It is the evil servant who falls into the trap of saying, "My master is not returning for a long time." Of course it is not just the spoken word or thought of a disobedient servant that is concerning. It is also a lifestyle lived out of this expectation, whether consciously or unconsciously. *I'm free to do as I please. My time is my own. I am the master of my destiny. I know the Master is returning, and I will respond when He does.* The sensible servant followed the master's instructions. The two types of servants presented by the story are easy to identify. Few servants are clearly one or the other. What is far more difficult is when the sensible servant begins to pick up characteristics of the evil servant. The mixture is hard to notice at first. Neglect of some of the Master's instructions begins to creep in. A rationalization for this perceived neglect is offered. After all, it is not really neglect, or so we are told. It is simply a change in focus. Morals change with supposed enlightenment. Resources need to be spent differently. However, neglect is neglect. The Master knows His instructions. The servant should know them, too. They are in the book. All servants have this potential to be self-deceived. The heart is desperately wicked (Jer. 17:9). Therefore watch and pray.

Fourth, if the return of Christ is completely mysterious and unknowable or filled with hypothetical outcomes, you should be skeptical. An uncertain or unknowable return is much like a far away, in the future, return. It will not have an impact on behavior nor encourage watchfulness. Rather, the return of Jesus is a *certain uncertainty*. And we are told to know the times. The season will arrive with appropriate further instructions. The clarity needed for that season will be released. If no one is watching, then no one will get ready.

They will find other things to do—good or bad, better or best—and will ultimately experience the Master's displeasure when He returns.

Fortunately, God has provided a helpful analogy for the mysterious return—birth. Paul used the analogy of birth to describe the last days (1 Thess. 5:3). Pregnancy should be obvious to almost all. Labor has an expected yet somewhat surprising start, with uneven contractions at first. The contractions steadily increase and grow in severity, with fewer and fewer rest periods in between until the crowning moment and birth—with no escape. The day of the Lord, or season of the Bridegroom God, will have this flavor—obvious pregnancy, labor expectations, contractions, periods of rest, faster and more intense contractions with less rest between events, and then the bride will be ready and free from all her adversaries. It would be rare, indeed, for a woman to wake up and find herself bewildered by a baby in her arms.

There is still time to change a measure of the outcome. There is a promise of help. Restoration of the House of Prayer may need a bump to overcome the inertia of business-as-usual Christianity and Judaism. Contractions will provide that necessary bump. But it is a thoughtful and calculated bump, designed to change hearts and awaken the sleeping Bride. Ignoring the signs will not avert the pains of birth. For those who have ignored all God's warnings and live in complete denial, the end will be a horrific surprise.

Fifth, if your view requires complex theological or technical explanations, you should be troubled. The vast majority of saints down through the ages were not well educated and literate. They were simple folks looking for a visible return and the beginning of a new era. This is the primary audience for the scriptures. The more convoluted the explanation, the more likely key information is still missing. Too much conjecture or too little should be concerning.

Last, if your view implies that you should gather your supplies, head for the hills, and hunker down until the trouble passes, you should pause. While the general maxim, "It's going to get darker before it gets lighter" is often quoted, it misses the mark of the last days. The day of the Lord is coming. However, it will be both terrible and marvelous at the same time (Joel 2:11). It will not be one followed by the other, but both; and it is not sequential as we tend to think, but in concert. It isn't possible to hide from one and await the other. The day of the Lord will not simply be a season of doom and gloom followed by fair skies. Isaiah's dawn will rise and will gain ascendency (Isaiah 60:1-3). The night will get darker and darker for those who love darkness and more desperate in its competition with light until it is removed by the overwhelming light of Jesus which will remain and carry into the age to come.

Prayer that drives God's government will gain dominance. It will not drop off during the time of the last days. There will be martyrs and the antichrist will have a small measure of control and victory for a time (Rev. 13:17), but signs and wonders (David's awesome deeds) and a great harvest (Acts 15:17) will break out all around him! The strong man's house (Matt. 12:29) will be raided all over the world. John's revelation actually presents the account of the collapse of Satan's kingdom. Today's saints seem to gloss over the growing glory of this time. Satan cannot shut it down or push it down a different path.

Gentile believers must understand what will befall Israel so that they can pray effectively in God's House. How will God resolve ancient animosity between Jews and Christians? They will both discover Jesus. He will give them an assignment that will only work if they participate together, where the payoff is so much greater than either can accomplish on their own—the House of Prayer: intimacy and the drawing of the nations.

C. S. Lewis, in the first of his Chronicles of Narnia children's stories, may have provided one of the best illustrations of the last days. *The Lion, The Witch and the Wardrobe* takes place in a kingdom where it is always winter and never Christmas. The kingdom is controlled by an iron-fisted wicked witch. But Aslan, the Christ figure, is on the move, and the witch's kingdom begins to crumble. Christmas comes with great joy, and the winter snow and ice continue their melt and yield to spring. The witch is still potent and does all she can to regain her kingdom and put the freeze back, but it continues to slip through her fingers. Spring is relentless, and the creatures she has captured and frozen during her reign are restored and enter the final battle against her. She gathers all her remaining armies and confederates, but Aslan handily defeats her nonetheless, and the celebration that started with the thaw and coming of Father Christmas goes into high gear. Don't run and hide. Look up!

Be alert. Pray. Sharath the Lord. Sharath Israel. "Arise, shine; for your light has come, And the glory of the LORD has risen upon you" (Isa. 60:1).

Although the release of the House of Prayer according to Amos is tied to Israel and the last days, it might be tempting to think the focus on the House of Prayer is a modern invention—a forced interpretation with no historical prece-dent. Not so. The next chapter will explore this.

Chapter Twenty

BEYOND THE NEW TESTAMENT

Acts 15 promised a restoration of the fallen tabernacle of David. It would be a *last days* phenomenon. Throughout the history of the church, threads or distinctive elements of the House of Prayer that David chronicled can be found. Like the New Testament witness, there is no continuous or enduring Davidic intercession that biblical historians can point to in a clear and unambiguous way. The church did not universally embrace Davidic intercession when it finally had the power to do so. It wasn't normative for that time period but its restoration was coming. It had a future destiny. It needed to be restored.

There are, however, groups and time periods when Davidic intercession was clearly on the minds of some, and in this chapter, we will look at some highlights. Scholars up to this point have not been looking for Davidic intercessory footprints in history. As the last days reality picks up steam and interest in Davidic worship grows, other well-documented historical accounts will likely surface as well.

Christianity grew in spite of Roman persecution, and in fact used the Roman roads and territory to expand, eventually moving outside of Roman-controlled areas. This chapter touches church history with a limited and narrow focus. It is not an attempt to tell the church's story in detail. Many other sources exist that document its progress from the time of the apostles. This chapter surveys evidence of House of Prayer thinking and a flavor of its impact in the three major arms of Christianity that we recognize today. The vast majority of Christians fall into one of three branches: the Roman Catholic Church, the collection of Orthodox churches, and the broadly diverse assortment of Protestant churches. A testimony to the House of Prayer can be found in each.

In the Roman Catholic West, Sigismund established a monastery in AD 515 (Abbey of Saint-Maurice d'Agaune), sixty-four kilometers due east of Geneva. A key feature of its liturgy was *laus perennis*—perpetual praise (prayer). The monks divided up into companies called *turmae*, and one company would replace another company throughout the day and night.

Barbara Rosenwein, an historian, notes, "There had been nothing like it in the West before, and even after it would be associated with Agaune. Only a decade or so later, Saint Benedict's Rule would allot about four hours a day to the liturgy. To historians, Saint-Maurice's round of prayer seems an aberration" (Farmer, Rosenwein, Monks & Nuns, Saints and Outcasts: Religion in Medieval Society 2000, 40). Day and night was simply too much and was reduced to four hours. The unusual *laus perennis* was thought to have come from Constantinople in the Orthodox East and monasteries of the *Acoemeti*. Davidic worship, it would seem, was simply not mainstream in the west.

Alexander Akimites was a fifth century monk in Constantinople—modern day Istanbul—who established his monastery around AD 430. *Acoemetus* means *sleepless ones*. The Psalmist said he meditated on the law day and night (Ps. 1:2), and this became a capstone verse to the *Akoemeti,* as they were known. Alexander divided the monks into choirs, and they rotated throughout the twenty-four-hour period in continual song. David himself would cry out to the Lord morning, noon and night (Ps. 55:16-19) while the Levitical singers *sharathed* the Lord continuously (1 Chron. 16:37) each day. Initially, those associated with Akimites were considered as social deviants and driven outside the capitol. There were likely many reasons the Akimites were shunned in the beginning, but 24/7 Davidic worship has a history of stops and starts and opposition. By the middle of the fifth century, the *Acoemeti* had become very orthodox but were still peculiar. Rosenwein notes:

> Alexander's biographer calls the result (in modern Latin translation) *assidua hymnodia* or *perennis hymnologia.* This is fundamentally equivalent to *laus perennis,* since a hymn was a song of praise. But the precise term *laus perennis*—at least when used to refer to a liturgical round, even to that of the *Acoemeti*—seems to be a modern construct. (Farmer, Rosenwein, Monks & Nuns, Saints and Outcasts: Religion in Medieval Society 2000, 42)

Rosenwein continues:

> No contemporary sixth-century source dealing with *Agaune* speaks of its *laus perennis*; those words were simply never used. Contemporaries spoke instead of its psalmody, which lasted through both night and day: it was *assiduous psalmody* or *hymns of psalmody day and night* or *divine songs by day and night* or *psalmody by turmae both night and day*, and so on. (Ibid. 2000, 40)

In other words, *perpetual praise,* as a phrase, was too general. It was a modern construct and left behind its Davidic reference point: night and day, 24/7. A strong connection between the *Acoemeti* and *Agaune* has not been established in the available documents. There were certainly conversations between Eastern and Western leaders, and this may well be the connection, but it is also possible the two functioned somewhat independently of each other. The witness of the House of Prayer had been planted in both East and West in a measure but did not thrive and become mainstream with one notable exception.

Laus perennis also appeared in Ireland, and this turned out to have a very large evangelistic impact across Europe, as David would have expected. According to Adamson and tradition, Saint Patrick came upon a certain valley, and it was reported that he and his companions "beheld the valley filled with a heavenly light and with a multitude of the host of heaven they heard, as chanted forth from the voice of angels, the psalmody of the celestial choir" (Adamson 2010, accessed December 2010). The place became known as the

Valley of the Angels and later the monastery of Bangor was built there by Comgall. Saint Patrick may well have encountered the heavenly House of Prayer that will be considered in the next chapter.

Ireland lay outside the Roman world at the time of Patrick (AD 430). His grandfather had been a priest, and his father was a *curialis*—one who collected taxes for the empire. As such, Patrick could have looked forward to a middle-class life and classical Latin education. His family lived somewhere along the west coast of Romanized Briton. Whatever dreams he may have had were dashed when, as a young boy, he was kidnapped by Irish slave traders. From the available accounts, it is easy to see that life as a slave was miserable. He eventually escaped, became a priest, and went back to Ireland as a missionary. His work was very successful, but with the fall of the Roman Empire, law and order had begun to crumble. A local British king attacked an Irish village, killing many and carrying off some of Patrick's converts. When Patrick heard what had happened, he was outraged and wrote to the priests in the king's fiefdom. However, "the British Christians did not recognize the Irish Christians either as full-fledged Christians or as human beings—because they were not Roman" (Cahill, How The Irish Saved Civilization 1995, 112). Racism has a long history.

Irish believers were different: Rough and ready; coming out of a pagan tradition filled with unsavory vice rather than converts from the somewhat domesticated Roman world. Cahill, reflecting on Matthew 11:12 and the parable of the violent taking the kingdom by force, gave this comment:

> In the Gospel story, the passionate, the out-
> sized, the out-of-control have a better shot
> at seizing heaven than the contained, the
> calculating, and those of whom this world
> approves. Patrick, indeed, seems to have
> been attracted to the same kinds of oddball,
> off-center personalities that attracted Jesus,
> and this attraction alone makes him unusual
> in the history of churchman. (Cahill, How
> The Irish Saved Civilization 1995, 123)

Cahill could just as easily have put David in his quote rather than Patrick. These Irish converts and others drove the monastery of Bangor, Ireland. At its height, 3,000 monks lived there. They were broken into three companies. Each took an eight-hour shift to pursue *laus perennis*. Their antiphonal style of praise and intercession lasted almost 300 years, until the monastery was eventually destroyed by invading Vikings in AD 824. As the Roman world disintegrated and the barbarians took the upper hand, it was the Irish who came to Europe's aid. The impact of the resulting outreach from Bangor was considerable. Two famous sons of Bangor are St. Molua and St. Columbanus. The *Ulster Journal of Archeology* gives the following summary. Bernard of Clairvaux (AD 1090-1153) coming some 300 years after the fall of Bangor wrote:

> A place it was, truly sacred, the nursery of
> saints who brought forth fruit most abun-
> dantly to the Glory of God, insomuch that
> one of the sons of that holy congregation,

Molua by name, is alone reputed to have been the founder of *a hundred monasteries:* which I mention for this reason, that the reader may, from this single instance, form a conception of the number to which the community amounted. In short, so widely had its branches extended through Ireland and Scotland that these times appear to have been especially foreshadowed in the verses of *David* . . . Nor was it only into the countries I have mentioned but even into distant lands that crowds of saints, like an inundation, poured. One of whom, St. Columbanus, penetrating into these our regions of France, built the monastery of Luxeuil and there became a great multitude. (Ulster Archaeological Society website, accessed December 2010)

The British priests' response to Patrick was sad, but highlights a gospel challenge. The gospel was not a call to embrace Roman culture and Roman Christianity. The Irish came with a fresh outlook and approach. Richardson writes:

Roman Christians preached, called for a decision, and then began churches when people believed. Celtic Christians, in contrast, invited people into their monastic communities to belong before they believed. Celtic monasteries were colonies of laypeople devoted to *prayer,* discipline, practical love, evangelism and hospitality. Religious brothers and sisters went out in teams to befriend pre-Christian people to serve and communicate Christian faith through conversations, analogies and stories. (Richardson, Evangelism Outside The Box 2000, 59)

It is not too difficult to connect the dots. The Irish missions outreach to Europe followed their Bangor practice. *Laus perennis*, or more correctly 24/7 Davidic worship, anchored their evangelism and communities. David would have been pleased to see Houses of Prayer impacting communities and reaching the lost. The pagan could come and find help in both spiritual and natural realms. He could see a blacksmith, get direction from a carpenter, learn better farming techniques, see night and day worship and intercession, and discover Jesus.

The literature shows examples of 24/7 Davidic-like intercession in both the Orthodox and Roman Catholic traditions but they did not become mainstream.

Another high point in the life of the House of Prayer came in the eighteenth century amongst Protestants. When the church became mired down in the sixteenth and seventeenth centuries, *prayer societies* appeared. These biweekly prayer meetings grew in prevalence and significance as God maneuvered His church for an historic outreach. Count Zinzendorf's Moravians followed and were united in prayer, even though their backgrounds were diverse. A Moravian account of this stirring for prayer as cited by Geoff Waugh is as follows:

On 5 August the Count spent the whole night in prayer with about twelve or fourteen others following a large meeting for prayer at midnight where great emotion prevailed. On Sunday, 10 August, Pastor Rothe, while leading the service at Herrnhut, was overwhelmed by the power of the Lord about noon. He sank down into the dust before God. So did the whole congregation. They continued till midnight in prayer and singing, weeping and praying.

On Wednesday, 13 August 1727, the Holy Spirit was poured out on them all. Their prayers were answered in ways far beyond anyone's expectations. Many of them decided to set aside certain times for continued earnest prayer. On 26 August, twenty-four men and twenty-four women covenanted together to continue praying in intervals of one hour each, day and night, each hour allocated by lots to different people. On 27 August, this new regulation began. Others joined the intercessors and the number involved increased to seventy-seven. They all carefully observed the hour which had been appointed for them. The intercessors had a weekly meeting where prayer needs were given to them. (Waugh 2011, accessed April 2011)

Astoundingly, this commitment to cover each twenty-four-hour period with prayer continued for over 100 years. The commitment to pray 24/7, the mixing of song and prayer, and scheduling by lot is an echo of Davidic worship. This Moravian movement grounded in prayer is considered to be the catalyst for the eighteenth century Protestant missionary revival around the world. It appears both full-time missionaries as well as laity participated with strong community support. Protestant revivals that followed in subsequent centuries would always point to the Moravian prayer movement as the driving agent. However, in the protestant world as well, Davidic worship did not yet become mainstream.

But there is good news! The second half of the 20th century has seen an explosion of prayer venues including Houses of Prayer (USA), Watchman Calls (Germany), Revival Prayer Houses (India), Hours of Praise and Worship; 24/7 Prayer (England), Prayer Watches (South Africa) as well as Prayer Towers (India) and Prayer Mountains in South Korea (Przybylski 2015, accessed April 2020). Davidic worship continues to appear around the world in the modern period and is now gaining momentum. God continues to bear witness to what He showed David, and it would appear that its full restoration is near. The missions organizations of the world are beginning to recognize the need for Houses of Prayer in reaching the lost and finishing the great commission. Some of the largest missions organizations today are collectively asking God to double the number of churches in the earth by 2020. To do this, they are also asking God to raise up 740,000 Houses of Prayer (Anderson 2012). They are seeking to establish a House of Prayer in every language and people group in the earth (Bickle 2013) as they pray and work toward the final push in Bible translation. The 2020 target date has been moved out but the associated need for houses of prayer is telling. David would be pleased. They are driven by Luke's passionate description in Acts 15 of that great, final drawing of all mankind, the coming great harvest. The House of Prayer is not just a tactical solution, but it is also strategic. And it appears to be how heaven runs.

Chapter Twenty-One

THE HEAVENLY
HOUSE OF PRAYER

T he apostle John was given a glimpse of the heavenly House of Prayer in chapters four and five of his Revelation. It came after Jesus's evaluation of the seven citywide churches in chapters two and three, but before the colossal seal, trumpet, and bowl judgments and the full restoration of the bride. The bridge between the sin-encrusted bride and the bride who has made herself ready is the House of Prayer. Here is what John sees.

> Around the throne were twenty-four thrones; and upon the thrones *I saw* twenty-four elders sitting, clothed in white garments, and golden crowns on their heads ... and before the throne *there was something* like a sea of glass, like crystal; and in the center and around the throne, four living creatures full of eyes in front and behind. (Rev. 4:4-6)

There were twenty-four elders, perhaps representing both believing Israel and the apostles. The city of Revelation

21:13-14 had the twelve foundation stones for the apostles; the layout of the gates matched the formation of Israel around the tabernacle. There are three tribes on each side for a total of twelve (Num. 2). Both Gentiles and Jews are called to *sharath* the Lord! The white garments are the righteous acts of the saints (Rev. 19:8).

> And the four living creatures, each one of them having six wings, are full of eyes around and within; and day and night they do not cease to say, HOLY, HOLY, HOLY is THE LORD GOD, THE ALMIGHTY, WHO WAS AND WHO IS AND WHO IS TO COME. (Rev. 4:8)

The description of Revelation 4:6-8 has features reminiscent of both Ezekiel and Isaiah. The cherubim (Ex. 25:20) that are shown with wings raised over the mercy seat of the Ark and facing the mercy seat are suggestive of the seraphim or living creatures of Revelation 4 that are around the throne of heaven. They may be different winged creatures, but their proximity to and posture before the throne is clear. They keep their eyes on God and worship Him day and night.

> And when the living creatures give glory and honor and thanks to Him who sits on the throne, to Him who lives forever and ever, the twenty-four elders will fall down before Him who sits on the throne, and will worship Him who lives forever and ever, and will cast their crowns before the throne,

> saying, Worthy are You, our Lord and our
> God, to receive glory and honor and power;
> for You created all things, and because of
> Your will they existed, and were created.
> (Rev. 4:9-11)

The *stephanos* or crown was given for running the race successfully (1 Pet. 5:4). Running well requires dedication—time, treasure, and talent. "Therefore I run in such a way, as not without aim; I box in such a way, as not beating the air" (1 Cor. 9:26). Yet the dedicated in the heavenly scene cast down their crowns and accomplishments—humility, the posture of the Davidic worshiper. Glory, honor, and thanks to Him were all found in 1 Chronicles 16—David's instructions to his singers.

> When He had taken the book, the four living
> creatures and the twenty-four elders fell
> down before the Lamb, each one holding
> a harp and golden bowls full of incense,
> which are the prayers of the saints. And
> they sang a new song, saying, Worthy are
> You to take the book and to break its seals;
> for You were slain, and purchased for God
> with Your blood *men* from every tribe and
> tongue and people and nation. (Rev. 5:8:9)

The prayers of the saints are the incense of the golden bowls, as David knew. Instrumentally (harp) assisted intercession (Rev. 5:8) is underway. Singing and speaking (declaring) were all in David's tent. Saints from every tribe and tongue are all the Jews and Gentiles who have been drawn by the Bridegroom God to salvation in His Son (John 6:44).

> You have made them *to be* a kingdom and priests to our God; and they will reign upon the earth. Then I looked, and I heard the voice of many angels around the throne and the living creatures and the elders; and the number of them was myriads of myriads, and thousands of thousands, saying with a loud voice, Worthy is the Lamb that was slain to receive power and riches and wisdom and might and honor and glory and blessing. (Rev. 5:10-12)

The saints are a kingdom, and they will reign on earth and be priests around the throne—just like David. Corporate intercession takes place when saints, angels, creatures, and elders are all joined together. It is loud and celebratory.

> And every created thing which is in heaven and on the earth and under the earth and on the sea, and all things in them, I heard saying, To Him who sits on the throne, and to the Lamb, *be* blessing and honor and glory and dominion forever and ever. And the four living creatures kept saying, Amen. And the elders fell down and worshiped. (Rev. 5:13:14)

Declarations about God, His character, and His worthiness are there, along with strong testimonies about who He is and what He has done. Statements about His dominion—His government and His reign—are declared. There is agreement in prayer. Amen, let it be so. This could be called the heavenly House of Prayer.

The bride, who had been represented by the seven Asian churches with a clouded testimony, is now changed. Her participation in the House of Prayer appears to make the difference.

> Then one of the elders answered, saying to me, These who are clothed in the white robes, who are they, and where have they come from? I said to him, My lord, you know. And he said to me, These are the ones who come out of the great tribulation, and they have washed their robes and made them white in the blood of the Lamb. For this reason, they are before the throne of God; and they serve Him day and night in His temple; and He who sits on the throne will spread His tabernacle over them. (Rev. 7:13-15)

The saints who come out of the great tribulation now have robes of white. They are now ready and can *serve* (*latreuo*) night and day in heaven. God will be *tenting* (*skene*) over them. God remains the day and night God. "And the devil who deceived them was thrown into the lake of fire and brimstone, where the beast and the false prophet are also; and they will be tormented day and night forever and ever" (Rev. 20:10). Satan and his accomplices, too, have a continuous day and night destiny.

And in the end, "There will no longer be any curse; and the throne of God and of the Lamb will be in it [Jerusalem], and His bond-servants will serve [latreuo] Him; they will see His face, and His name will be on their foreheads" (Rev. 22:3-4). It will be face-to-face *sharath*ing just like David saw.

The revelation of the House of Prayer is stunning, and it would be easy for the reader to stay stunned and not respond. The modern entertainment culture has helped condition us this way. Today's blockbuster movie thrills us, we leave the cinema intrigued, our hearts racing, and gladly await the next offering, which promises even greater thrills. Our lives, however, unfortunately remain unchanged. But God will not leave it this way. Moving the church into a House of Prayer heart and practice is daunting. It is not a small adjustment in our walk with Christ.

We are given a clue to God's process of change at the end of the age. "The LORD utters His voice before His army; Surely His camp is very great, For strong is he who carries out His word. The day of the LORD is indeed *great* [marvelous] and very *awesome* [fearful], And who can endure it (Joel 2:11)?

There will be negative pressure in society pushing the body of Christ closer to Him and His strategic plan. There will be marvels—signs and wonders—drawing the body into thankful, enjoyable intimacy in the midst of a world with growing chaos. These are the parameters that God is using. If this is God's plan, how should the body of Christ respond?

Chapter Twenty-Two

BRETHREN, WHAT
SHALL WE DO?

P eter's first sermon (Acts 2:14) had enormous impact
on the fledgling church. The brethren listening were
dumbfounded by the content, literally pierced to the heart,
and asked Peter how they should respond. If God is restoring
night and day prayer according to David, as suggested here,
it will have significant impact on the church. It is reasonable to assume that today's believers would ask a similar
question: "Lord, how do we respond to this?" Two answers
come to mind.

Believers must first adopt the Berean approach that
was introduced in Chapter Fourteen. The Bereans carefully
searched the scriptures to see if what the missionary Paul
presented was true (Acts 17:11). The revelation of Jesus
rocked Judaism, and a serious examination of the Bible was
essential. Today, it is easy to see Jesus in the Old Testament.
Two thousand years has given the church time to find and
digest most if not all the messianic references. This was not
the case in Paul's day. Jesus, the God man who died and rose
again was simply not on anyone's radar.

Likewise, when Martin Luther understood salvation by faith and William Seymour saw the work of the Holy Spirit in a new light, the entire church was profoundly affected. The potential impact of the restoration of the House of Prayer is not on the scale of the revelation of Jesus, but the implications are significant, far-reaching, and startling. It is in line with the impact of the rise of the Protestant Church in the sixteenth century and the Pentecostal movement in the twentieth century. What exactly are today's Berean believers being asked to consider?

God has an end of the age battle plan He is now releasing in the last days. In most competitions, strategy changes as one nears the finish line. Sometimes the shift in strategy is dramatic.

God not only wants to win—which most believers intuitively understand—but He wants to win big for His Son. His battle plan includes the restoration of one particular provision first given to King David as a commanded practice. It will put the game beyond reach of God's enemies. The enemy will scream and terrify, but the saints will triumph. Restoring this practice of night and day prayer will be a game changer. It will change the spiritual horizon.

David was given a divine plan for the creation and operation of God's House of Prayer. Heaven, in some dimension, has always run this way and will do so eternally, as the apostle John saw. In this season, His manifest presence, in the House of Prayer, will be released on earth in many locations of God's choosing, particularly cities.

The prominent feature of the House of Prayer is night and day corporate Davidic intercessory worship. Intimacy is its driving characteristic. Although the saints will be edified in the process (1 Cor. 14:26), edification is not the goal. God is its primary audience.

For an audience of one, believers throughout the world today are engaged in Davidic worship—the night and day corporate offering that mixes instrumentally supported worship and intercession before the face of the Lord, according to the heavenly pattern given King David. The *sharath* of the Lord—the sacrificial service *to* the Master from a cleansed, humble and intimate heart that generates the remarkable, delightful and deeply satisfying experience *of* the Master— is growing daily. First commandment Davidic worship will drive His missions outreach to the nations with awesome deeds and a massive harvest.

David is God's witness to the peoples—the gold standard or divine example. He was zealous and dedicated to the House of Prayer; willing to suffer ridicule over God's things; sometimes depressed or hard pressed, yet singing and declaring almost always; participating morning, noon and night as best he could in spite of his busy schedule. It was his one thing desire. He loved being there, and when not there, he was longing to be there (Ps. 61).

In David's day, it was manned full time by Levitical singers and musicians who were fully supported, but in the last days, it will be manned principally by foreign intercessors—Gentile worshipers of Jesus. They will give God no rest until He makes Jerusalem a praise in all the earth (Isa. 62:6-7)—a place of worship, a place of salvation, provision, enjoyment and much more. Some Davidic intercessory worshipers will be dedicated to the ministry and fully funded in some fashion, but many, perhaps most, will be volunteers. They will cry out for the restoration of the church and its mission. A fiery church will in turn collectively and earnestly begin to cry out for the restoration of Israel and summation of God's purposes for the earth. This includes an enormous end time revival, larger than anything previously seen delivered by a passionate God with awesome deeds.

The House of Prayer will also be an unusual place of refuge, a place designed for the righteous who recognize their need for clean hands and who long to encounter the God who forgives and restores. It will be a place of individual and corporate repentance in seasons of great difficulty. The cry for help will move heaven. It will be a place to experience the delights of God and gain insight into His revelation. It will be a place of provision and a place for the nations to come and discover God and His mercy, deliverance, healing, and salvation.

It will also be the strength of a city. Its spiritual location will be on the wall of the city—holding the gates, focusing on what is coming to the city that should be resisted or welcomed, and focusing also on what is happening in the city that likewise requires remedy or thanksgiving as the case may be. The prosperity of the city in that day will be linked to the House of Prayer's operation. It may be in one location within a given city or several locations, but it will be organized for 24/7 operation and follow the standards established by David.

It could be argued that everything the House of Prayer can bring to the table is present in the existing ministries of the church and parachurch organizations today. Yet God purposed to restore the House of Prayer. Why? The last days appear to be a time when evil and righteousness are turbo-charged for a climactic end of the age finale. Is it possible

Brethren, What Shall We Do?

the House of Prayer brings an added dimension, a mighty boost to strengthen righteousness, intimacy, and power more than commensurate with the attack of evil that Satan plans? God intends to win big and show His glory.

Secondly, we take Mary's response to heart when the angel Gabriel came and announced that she would have a son supernaturally. The implications were not lost on Mary. In the end, Mary said, "Behold, the bondslave of the Lord; may it be done to me according to your word" (Luke 1:38). Like Mary, we realign our expectations and agree with heaven's plans.

Berean Strategies

Berean investigators have at least three hurdles to overcome in their scriptural evaluation of the House of Prayer summary provided above. There is, first of all, a great deal of tradition and theology already in place today that may cloud the evaluation. Both tradition (how we have always done things) and theology (our consensus on the Bible's message) can be very helpful, but they can also hamper a fresh look at the scriptures that will be required. Tradition and theology are not inspired. They are manmade, age over time, and must always be held up to the scriptures—the plumb line of our faith.

It is possible to corrupt the delivery and understanding of God's words, either intentionally or unintentionally, and produce odd theology and practice (tradition). Jesus had a great deal to say to those who handled God's words. The Pharisees, scribes, and lawyers all mistreated God's words. They happily embraced some and intentionally neglected others. This will always lead to poor tradition and theology and God's correction.

> You do not have His word abiding in you,
> for you do not believe Him whom He sent.
> You search the Scriptures because you think
> that in them you have eternal life; it is these
> that testify about Me; and you are unwilling
> to come to Me so that you may have life.
> (John 5:38-40)

They certainly knew a great deal of God's Word, but it didn't live in them. They appeared righteous, but their hearts were crooked. A crooked heart will lead to a crooked evaluation of God's words and misdirection for those who follow them.

The office of the priest in Jesus's day was no better. "Then the chief priests and the elders of the people were gathered together in the court of the high priest, named Caiaphas; and they plotted together to seize Jesus by stealth and kill Him" (Matt. 26:3-4). Elements of *external sharath*ing were present in the days of Caiaphas. Handling all the sacrifices and aspects of the temple celebration and feasts required a certain dedication and skill. Nevertheless, the office, like the handling of God's Word, had become corrupted. It looked good on the outside but was rotten on the inside. The deep satisfaction that both the jailer and Potiphar received in Joseph's *sharath*ing was absent from God's experience. Jesus had to cleanse the temple. His House of Prayer had been rezoned for commercial activity. Some of the form was there. The substance was not. The risk is real that the heart can disappear and leave behind a good appearance or tradition but empty practice or downsized obedience, as Malachi noted.

Jesus used very strong language to rebuke their lifestyle and handling of His words. Jesus noted, "Whoever then annuls one of the least of these commandments, and teaches others *to do* the same, shall be called least in the kingdom of heaven; but whoever keeps and teaches *them*, he shall be called great in the kingdom of heaven" (Matt. 5:19). The religious leaders did not receive Jesus or recognize David's command to *sharath* the Lord as Hezekiah and Josiah had done.

Paul successfully passed on his presentation of Jesus the Messiah to the Bereans. Paul's testimony—what he believed (taught) and how he practiced it—was consistent even under careful scrutiny, and this in spite of the traditions and theology prevalent at the time. Paul still had to leave town when Jews of Thessalonica came stirring up and agitating the crowds (Acts 17:13). The fact that the Messiah had come and gone left everyone on tilt. Theology and practice were appropriately shaken and the plumb line rechecked. Some responded joyfully, and some became murderous. No doubt every feeling in between was represented in Paul's audiences. Berean, beware.

The second and perhaps greater challenge today's Berean saints face is overcoming the redefinition of biblical concepts to match modern expectations and experience. Theology and tradition are not normally hidden. Redefinition of biblical concepts, however, is subtle and develops slowly over time to avoid confrontation and being unmasked.

Prayer, for example, is not mainly a transaction for obtaining services when all other avenues of support have been exhausted, as the church practice seems to indicate. That isn't prayer. Rather, it is as David shared—intimate, relational, consuming, sometimes inconvenient yet full of life; fully engaged whether in trials or triumphs. God does provide when we ask (James 4:1-3), but heart and relationship are crucial.

Faith, too, like prayer, has been redefined. It is not exclusively an individual and private practice, as a modern audience might believe. Nor is it solely the practice of a likeminded congregation. We are part of a body with Jesus as the head. David gave prayer an important corporate, city-wide dimension that can't be neglected without doing significant harm to biblical faith and prayer. Adopting biblical language while changing the content is a grave pitfall. Tying ourselves to the scriptures, context and content, is more than wise. It will be critical in the days ahead. The atmospheric white noise of religious nonsense will be acute in these last days. False prophets will peddle half-truths or no truth (Matt. 7:15). And God Himself will send a deluding influence among those who do not love the truth (2 Thess. 2:9-12). Redefinition is silent and insidious. A humble love of the truth will hold us steady.

Related to the redefinition of Bible concepts is the adoption of new language. This is a third challenge to Bereans. It might seem appropriate to call the church to a *culture of prayer*, but new open terminology can mean anything we want. There is no measure for success or failure. It may be positive language and descriptive of what we think is needed, but in the end it is like a vapor—here for a moment and passing away. The words of scripture are inspired and firmly established and won't move. The church needs the night and day House of Prayer as David gave it. The Bereans wouldn't let go of the scriptures. They received the Word with joy, not skepticism, and searched to confirm what they had received. Assuming the Berean due diligence has occurred, it is essential to get a read on what is done today. Going on a journey assumes you know where you are going and where you are now before starting out.

Few Christians would doubt the foundational aspect of prayer in the practice of their faith. But do we really pray? The church has many bright spots today, but the Western church in particular actually prays very little. The idea of prayer is revered in the church, and evangelicals believe they are praying, but the actual practice is but a whisper. E. M. Bounds wrote, "No learning can make up for the failure to pray. No earnestness, no diligence, no study, no gifts will supply its lack" (Bounds 2010, accessed December 2010). Repentance, albeit humbling, is an appropriate response to prayerlessness, individually and corporately.

In his 1962 book on prayer and revival, Leonard Ravenhill lamented:

> Where, oh, where are the tears over this lust-bound age of sinners, over the lost millions in heathen lands and over the cultured pagans on our own doorsteps? We would like to weep, but we are too busy and at the moment have too much of the dust of Time in our eyes to get the tears of Eternity moving. Yet if we are ever going

> to sow the seed of effective praying, the
> tears are going to flow. (Ravenhill, Revival
> praying 1962, 70)

He grieved over the absence of believing prayer in his generation. More solid support for his apprehension would come fifty years later. Application of night and day prayer according to David assumes you have some sense of where you are today.

The Pew Forum, a polling organization, based on their sampling has provided the following categorization of religious interest. It sorted...

> American adults into seven cohesive, like-
> minded groups based on the religious and
> spiritual beliefs they share, how actively
> they practice their faith, the value they
> place on their religion, and the other
> sources of meaning and fulfillment in their
> lives. (Pew Forum website 2018, accessed
> December 19, 2019)

They found that 84 percent of those described as *Sunday Stalwarts* pray daily. Those who identified as *Religious Resisters* and *Solidly Secular* taken together pray daily 12 percent of the time. What prayer looks like for the two previous groups is a mystery. However, those praying daily represented 44 percent of the sample. At first glance, this seems hopeful. The church in the West is praying something in some measure.

Unfortunately, all is not well in Western prayer. In a 2001 survey on faith practices based on a random sample of 1,005 adults in the US, George Barna, another polling organization, found that 82 percent had prayed to God in the last seven days (Barna 2001, accessed August 2011). This was in line with the Pew *Sunday Stalwarts* results. However, when the group was asked about private time to pray and read the Bible over the same period, only 49 percent found time to do so. And only 16 percent found time to attend a small group whose focus was on Bible study and prayer (Barna 2001, accessed August 2011). The discipline of developing a testimony and a corporate lifestyle of prayer looks very weak.

In a survey of professional clergy drawn largely from the United Kingdom, John Preston reported, "On average, respondents claim to spend about seven minutes a day in private prayer. When the Sample is re-adjusted to reflect the whole churchgoing population, the daily prayer time is reduced to about *four minutes*" (Preston 2004, accessed December 2010, emphasis added).

Three thousand church leaders from a range of denominations were invited to take part in the project. This was a very healthy sample size and composition. Twenty-five hundred were UK churches, with 500 churches from Australia, New Zealand, Canada, and the US. Preston received 5,644 completed surveys from 344 churches or 11 percent, with an average of sixteen surveys per church. Preston noted,

> Data supplied on congregation sizes suggests that 16 surveys per church represent around 13 percent of church members. Comparing these figures with other research

suggests these 13 percent are almost certainly skewed to those church members who pray more." (Preston 2004, accessed December 2010)

Preston commented on the reported four-minute average: "This seems relatively high, although it is influenced by a small number of people spending an hour or more in prayer each day, and by some respondents possibly overstating the time they spend praying" (Preston 2004, accessed December 2010). If the four-minute average is on the high side, then growing intimacy with God on this diet is not likely to occur. The sin of prayerlessness remains.

Other research sampled suggested that Preston's findings were close to reality. In the article, *Barna Reviews Top Religious Trends of 2005*, Barna looked at the priorities embraced by church leaders. He assumed the greater the declared priority, the greater the resource dollar spending on that priority would be. He argued that ministry to children, ministry to families, and prayer are essential to the life of the church, and these should be reflected in the stated priorities of the church. Only one in five Protestant churches viewed the ministry to family and children as a top priority; and with respect to prayer he noted, "Prayer ... is labeled one of the top priorities by less than one out of every twenty-five churches" (Barna 2005, accessed December 2010). If time, treasure, and talent make up the available resource spending for any given person or collectively for any given church and less than one in twenty-five churches emphasizes the importance of prayer, then one wonders what happens when 84 percent *Sunday Stalwarts*—who likely believe the scriptures—say they pray daily. This disconnect is glaring!

If prayer is revered and considered to be a daily practice, but there is little actual personal or clergy prayer and few churches even have a stated goal to pray, then moving to a House of Prayer practice is monumental. It would not be a simple adjustment to an existing lifestyle.

Barna noted in a 2004 survey, "Less than half of the public is strongly convinced of the position they hold on most of the core spiritual perspectives we evaluate" (Barna 2004, accessed December 2010). They have no testimony, no conviction. Declaring that prayer is a priority is not the same thing as aggressively advocating for it, funding it, or even doing it. How has the Western evangelical church fared as a whole with what appears to be a prayerless diet? In 2004, Barna commented on the American experience: "The survey discovered that evangelical Christians constitute just 7 percent of the adult population, which is statistically equivalent to the 6 percent measured in 1995" (Barna 2004, accessed December 2010). In short, the number of evangelicals, who in theory believe the book and embrace the need for prayer, is not growing.

Having a measurably weak prayer priority is a problem that goes beyond the evangelical or Protestant world. It affects Roman Catholics as well. The Catholic Communities of Prayer website provided the following John Paul II quote: "Our communities must become genuine 'schools' of prayer where the meeting with Christ is expressed not just in imploring help but also in thanksgiving, praise, adoration, contemplation, listening, and ardent devotion, until the heart truly 'falls in love'" (Catholic Communities of Prayer website, accessed January 2011). The Pope provided a clear testimony on the need for community prayer. However, in 2009, a survey was conducted across the archdioceses in the US. The Diocesan Appeal Campaigns from thirty-two archdioceses, reflecting 1,972 ministries, offices, services, and organizations, were reviewed. "There was not one prayer related ministry that was financially supported through this agency!" (Catholic Communities of Prayer website, accessed January 2011). As Barna described previously, following the resource spending reveals true priorities. Prayer is clearly part of the religious language for Roman Catholics, Protestants, and the general American public, but its serious practice in the West seems to be missing.

Marketing what is considered to be a new product is always challenging. How do you market a product to a market segment that believes they already have the product and use it regularly when the market research shows clearly that the product is not widespread and if present, is hardly used at all? Without God's help, it is a daunting task.

There are other indications that prayer in the West is weak. In a contemporary article for *Christianity Today*, Drew Dyck addressed the serious issue of declining church membership rolls. In his article, "The Leavers: Young Doubters Exit the Church," he wrote, "The answer, of course, lies in more than offering another program. Nor should we overestimate the efficacy of slicker services or edgy outreach. Only with prayer and thoughtful engagement will at least some of the current exodus be stemmed" (Dyck 2010, accessed December 2011, emphasis added).

In his article, Drew Dyck laments that young people—the future core of the church—are leaving or never even coming to church. He notes that the percentage of those in America who claim to have no religion has nearly doubled in just two decades. Twenty-two percent of those who reported no religion in the study he quotes were part of the twenty-somethings group (Ibid. 2010, accessed December 2011). But of even greater concern to Dyck than the general loss of religious interest in America was the number of young people who were simply dropping out of church.

He wrote, "According to Rainer Research, approximately 70 percent of American youth drop out of church between the age of eighteen and twenty-two. The Barna Group estimates that 80 percent of those reared in the church will be disengaged by the time they are twenty-nine" (Ibid. 2010, accessed December 2011). The reasons for this dire prediction of heavy decline are many, according to the author. De-conversion, as the phenomenon has been described, is getting lots of attention, but Drew Dyck's observation is more alarming still. If prayer is to be a major part of the solution, it is fair to assume the lack of prayer today helped produce the problem in the first place and continues to exacerbate the problem today. Not only is the product of prayer not being used, market share is shrinking dramatically as a result.

Naturally, it is easier to see problems as belonging to someone else. Completing your own survey may help. Take a typical week, divide the 168-hour week into fifteen-minute segments, and record how the time is being spent in a typical week. Summarize and review where the time went. A similar exercise can be done with finances. Take a typical month, and record income and expenses. How much was spent on charities, and of that, how much was spent on organizations that directly encourage and model prayer? As Barna noted, churches believe in prayer but typically don't spend their time or financial capital in prayer. You can't count your church tithe dollars as going toward prayer unless the church clearly supports, promotes, and spends its resources on prayer.

The Bureau of Labor Statistics compiled data in 2011 and suggested that working adults with children have 210 minutes of discretionary time each day—270 if they have no children (Bureau of Labor Statistics 2012, accessed May 28, 2016). No doubt, there would be plenty of disagreement over what constitutes discretionary time, but the average time in daily prayer, according to Preston, is still an overstated four minutes!

There is no escape. Today the saints of God, on average, spend 1,336 minutes each day on other things. A careful evaluation of where we are today is painful, but without a clear starting point and some understanding of the scope of what will be required, application of the scriptures will die before it gets started. The application for the churches is really the application of the collected individuals. Our practice today does not reflect what we say we believe. Leonard Ravenhill's lament was accurate. The charge of prayerlessness stands. Repentance, individually and corporately, is appropriate. However, House of Prayer help is on the way.

Assuming the scriptures have been handled correctly in this book and we have a broken heart for sin and prayerlessness and a rising hope for better things, then we can proceed. Fortunately, as David noted, God washes hands and hearts.

Lifestyle of Prayer

Armed with our going-in position, five general statements can now be made to help us move forward into a lifestyle of prayer. To begin with, what is done today in personal and corporate devotion is good and should be retained. This may sound like a contradiction, but it isn't. King Solomon responded to the Shulamite woman he planned to marry, "You have made my heart beat faster, my sister, *my* bride; You have made my heart beat faster with a single *glance* of your eyes, With a single strand of your necklace" (Song of Sol. 4:9). This is how God sees the saints. What we spend in devotion today is desperately small but still good. God loves the time with us even when it is highly abbreviated. He knows our frame. However, God wants to build intimacy and get us ready for His Son. This will take our time and attention. A course change is required. God wants more of our time, treasure, and talent—the total of who we are—and He wants us to invest differently for a different outcome.

Personal prayer, study, fellowship, and ministry are not going away or being replaced. Since everyone gets twenty-four hours a day and that number is fixed, the time that currently goes into other discretionary things must be reviewed, reprioritized, and/or dropped under the direction of the Holy Spirit, and a substantial measure redirected to the House of Prayer where hope awaits us. The writer of the book of Hebrews admonished the church. "Therefore, since we have so great a cloud of witnesses surrounding us, let us also lay aside every encumbrance and the sin which so easily entangles us, and let us run with endurance the race that is set before us" (Heb. 12:1). Encumbrances and sin must go to make room for the House of Prayer and God's investment strategy.

For David, regular religious observance at Gibeon was insufficient. Personal piety and communion, which David had, was insufficient. He had to have a public dwelling place for the Ark of God's presence (Ps. 132:5). Why? It was a dwelling place for the mighty one of Jacob. The mighty one was there and would stretch out His mighty hand. David wanted to get out of the way and let God do the heavy lifting and dividend building. David didn't simply get by. His investment (time, treasure, and talent) would go much further in God's hands.

God wants an invested heart that leans in by faith rather than a heart that leans out for fear of loss or a misplaced sense of security. God is a "very present help in trouble" (Ps. 46:1). The prophet Haggai reminded the saints of his day that though they were hard pressed in their personal lives, God's House was a greater priority. If they gave themselves to God's House, God Himself would provide what they needed, as David had seen.

The apostle Paul gained a similar investment revelation. He had what appeared to be a physical affliction, and he asked God three times to take it away. God said no, and He gave His economic equation to Paul. "And He has said to me, 'My grace is sufficient for you, for power is perfected in weakness.' Most gladly, therefore, I will rather boast about my weaknesses, so that the power of Christ may dwell in me" (2 Cor. 12:9). Paul caught on quickly. God was looking for weakness, voluntary and involuntary, what Paul chose for himself and what others chose for him. Weakness—the near exhaustion of resource—was music to God's ears.

When we expend ourselves and choose the lifestyle and behaviors of the kingdom of God and prefer those to our own personal kingdom welfare, even though outwardly this looks foolish and wasteful to the world, we will know God's power. The power and resources of the mighty one of Jacob will be well beyond what we can individually or corporately bring to the table. Paul was an astute apostle. David was a wise king.

When we pour out our lives for God and become weak, He will pour in His power. Voluntary acts of weakness include, but are not limited to, fasting, prayer, worship, study, giving, and other kingdom activities that require a measure of personal or corporate sacrifice. God is going to release outstanding power through His servants in the last days, but He does not wish to see His children corrupted by His powerful gifts. Consequently, He has determined to release His power in the context of our weakness and our lovesick devotion to Jesus.

Expending our strength in the prayer room will leave us weak and lacking in other areas of life and possibly lacking even in ministry, which will open the door for the power of God and, of course, reproach from others. David understood. He did not diversify and hedge his investment. He placed all that he had in God's hands. Jesus commended the widow who put her one cent into the temple treasury. It was all she had to live on, but Jesus, who was in His house, was watching (Mark 12:42-43). The widow was not foolish or reckless, but wise. One cent would not go far even in Jesus's day. It was a wise investment. Giving to God financially appears foolish, but God runs the kingdom, and He is able to pay great dividends on our investments.

The House of Prayer is such an investment that yields great dividends. David owned a home of cedar (1 Chron. 17:1) and raised a substantial family. It was not a call to poverty and destitution or a clever scheme to gain wealth through others to finance a lavish lifestyle, but a call to weakness so that the mighty one of Jacob would have a clear path to act according to His desire. The House of Prayer is an amazing last days investment strategy! Certainly a call to weakness can be abused, so wisdom is required. It is not a call to a monastic way of thinking or living. Nor is sloth a valid means of weakness. It is not a call to leave behind any of God's commandments in favor of a devotion expressed through the House of Prayer.

Secondly, this call for increased or extravagant resource spending and redirection mentioned above will lead to conflict. David's divine plan fundamentally disrupted the status quo. He called for an increase in resource spending across the nation—individually and corporately. (David needed 288 prophetic signers, 4,000 band members, and 4,000 gate keepers to run his tent.) He called himself and his nation to radical First Commandment pursuit and told his people the House of Prayer was core to God's plan—24/7 intercessory worship before God's face, in addition to what was already operating at Gibeon and in addition to the commands of Moses. It was around this core that other acts of necessary and valuable Second Commandment devotion, fellowship, outreach, and training, both corporate and individual, were to take place. The saints would need to make their human capital more available, and this would disrupt their carefully planned and managed personal experience. This is a recipe for conflict.

When human capital or supporting resources are in short supply, haggling for what is available takes place. Every business and individual operates this way. If you have only one dollar or one hour to spend, you must choose wisely how to spend it. If it is a single individual who has a dollar or hour to spend, then the haggling is all internal. When a group of people must decide how to spend that dollar or hour, there is a power struggle. He who owns the gold decides, but all the courtiers and influence peddlers jockey for position to make their opinion heard. Time is money, and money is power and control. It is not a casual process. The dynamic is true for individuals and groups.

Power, the ability to control the time, treasure, and talent of one person or many, is being challenged at some level. The House of Prayer will obviously not be received kindly in the realms of darkness. (Satan does not want a praying church.) But it also represents the potential for a significant shift in power in the natural where some will not receive it warmly either. To these, the House of Prayer threat must be neutralized.

Those who require human or other capital will fight to obtain and keep this resource for their operation. It may be dressed up in altruistic language, but the fundamentals are the same. "These are my people. This is my money. I'm in charge." The battle plan is simple. If the message can't be discounted, then the messenger will be discredited. This is a time-honored expected outcome, and another reason to count the cost and be certain of the scriptural veracity of the House of Prayer.

David's First Commandment posture understandably brought reproach. It was too much. It was over the top, too expensive, too invasive, and unrealistic. He became the song of drunkards (Ps. 69:10-12). The idea of 24/7 was preposterous and worthy of ridicule. No reasonable individual or corporate entity would give himself to this requirement. If God is behind the restoration of the House of Prayer as He was behind David, then David's personal House of Prayer experience will likely repeat itself among today's followers. The gauntlet has been thrown down. This dynamic must be understood. Adopting the House of Prayer will be a bumpy ride. Remember, you can't serve two masters (Matt. 6:24). We serve God or wealth.

Thirdly, the sky is not falling. This may also seem like another contradiction. The House of Prayer innovation may be badly needed, and to some, very late in arrival. However, there is time to change. Jesus is a good project manager and runs the universe very well. He is a lover and has provided ample time for His bride to transition before the last days really heat up and the need for the House of Prayer becomes truly urgent.

Our Western frame of thinking searches for quick solutions with no setbacks, please. We also want our results to be clear, measurable, and easily repeatable. Waiting, of course, is not like that, and the concept frustrates many in the West. An inability to wait may turn out to be the Western church's single greatest stumbling block to experiencing the House of Prayer. Because of impatience, some will conclude that prayer doesn't work and that the House of Prayer as a consumer of resources is wasteful. They will depart. They will return to what is familiar or look for another shiny object or program with promise. David's tent was not scientific: so much prayer effort and so much delay yields so much result.

It was, rather, relational and based on a person—a great person—God. And His ways are not our ways (Isa. 55:8). He seems to always walk on a road less traveled. Waiting will be required. And Jesus has planned for the necessary waiting!

In the business world, innovation is rarely embraced immediately. It takes time before it becomes widely recognized and adopted. And there is lots of scrutiny of the proposed product or process before it is accepted as an innovation and becomes mainstream. Waiting is involved. Change is always challenging and rarely popular at first. The restoration of the House of Prayer will operate like an innovation in the business world. (Of course, it is not really an innovation but rather, an ancient remedy.) There will be early adopters, those who say, "This is marvelous," as well as outspoken opposition—those who say, "This is dangerous." However, most saints will take a wait-and-see approach. And some will say no for a variety of reasons or no reason at all. They will conclude that the treatment of the scriptures presented in this book is flawed and likewise its conclusions.

Theology, tradition, denomination, culture, and numerous other factors affect our view, interpretation, and application of the scriptures. God's call to the church today to come back to prayer comes from a Davidic framework and isn't native to the modern church experience, whether Roman Catholic, Orthodox, or any variety of Protestant. And though it does not originate with any of these, it can be accommodated by all of them. An old practice that existed before the church is being given to the church. The House of Prayer doesn't replace the congregation. It can be one of many emphases within a congregation, or a primary focus of a congregation, or operate cross-congregationally as other ministries do today. Governance options would probably mirror what is used in churches and ministries today.

A House of Prayer heart and practice will take time before it gains general acceptance, and the first and critical step is the examination of the scriptures. If the case to adopt a House of Prayer lifestyle individually and corporately has not been successfully argued here, then no further action is required. Doing nothing is the right application. However, innovation, as noted above, requires scrutiny and careful examination. Much consideration often occurs before we become adopters. For this reason, if the House of Prayer message doesn't resonate with you today, set the book aside and wait for God to say more. We must have confidence in the biblical foundation of the House of Prayer before proceeding.

Gamaliel had it right. He rose up in the Sanhedrin in the early days of the church and warned his fellow leaders to do nothing concerning the activity of Peter and the healings occurring in Jerusalem (Acts 5:38-39). If the plan was from men rather than God, it would fail. If the House of Prayer is not being revived by God today, as asserted in this book, the current activity occurring around the world will not sustain itself. It will only be a fad, and a new fad is just around the corner, waiting to replace it. If it is from God, however, it will not disappear. And He will continue to lovingly woo and trumpet it.

Now, Jesus understands human nature as well (John 2:25). Procrastination and stubbornness were taken into consideration in His transition plan, and He will provide pressure to help transition as needed. Not everyone is an early adopter, majority adopter, or even a late adopter. The business model identifies a fourth group—laggards (Wikipedia, 2014). His plan accommodates all His servants—one way or another, even those who currently say, "No." He will court and invite even those. But the Father disciplines all His sons and daughters that He loves (Heb. 12:6) and will have His way.

Next, we must consider our roots. Paul had anguish in his heart over Israel. He had a very different perspective on Israel than what is commonly seen in the church today.

> I am telling the truth in Christ, I am not lying, my conscience testifies with me in the Holy Spirit, that I have great sorrow and unceasing grief in my heart. For I could wish that I myself were accursed, *separated* from Christ for the sake of my brethren, my kinsmen according to the flesh. (Rom. 9:1-3)

Paul did not abandon his Jewish roots. He did not minimize or marginalize the Old Testament. He saw the vine—Jesus—who supported the natural and wild branches. It is perhaps the greatest tragedy in the world that Israelites, who have such a deep heritage and have suffered so much, might actually miss Jesus and perish. By extension, we should also have sorrow for those in the church who are choosing unbelief in the face of God's mercy. They sit in the pew week by week but come no closer. Churchgoers and Jews look eerily similar. It is a family affair. Stubbornness runs deep. We have the same genes and pretty much the same historical patterns. Gentile believers must learn the family history and humbly guard their hearts. God never abandoned Israel, though He had plenty of reason to do so. To be brought near to God and reject Jesus is tragic. Any loss of life is tragic, but even more for those who have tasted a measure of God's goodness and still say no to Him. It is unbelievable and tragic. As John Bradford notes, "There but for the grace of God go I" (Bradford 1550, accessed May 2016).

The House of Prayer is to be manned by foreigners because Jews are temporarily blinded by unbelief. The way-wardness of Israel became the open door for gentiles, and now that gentiles are taking their place on the wall of night and day intercession, they can cry out for and *sharath* the older brother and participate in the family promises, provisions, and restoration. They can also cry out for the younger brother or prodigals who have been trapped in "every encumbrance and the sin which so easily entangles" (Heb. 12:1). Great compassion is needed.

Finally, David is our model for the House of Prayer. Check the label. If the label doesn't say, "According to David," then the designation *House of Prayer* may well mean something very different. The House of Prayer is not a euphemism for church as we understand it today. The House of Prayer's clearest definition, heart, and practice came from David. It was not a house of preaching, although preaching is good and necessary. It was not a house of fellowship and training, although these are profitable and must take place. It was not a house of programs, although programs can be very meaningful and encouraging. It was not even a house with worship events, although concerts of worship are delightful. It was about *sharath*ing the Lord. It was for Him. It was vertical in focus rather than horizontal, and it ran 24/7, not periodically. If the label is Davidic, check the underlying specifications provided in the scriptures. Davidic prayer had clear characteristics. Watch out for knockoffs. They look like the real thing, are usually less expensive, but normally don't deliver the value.

With this background, application can move forward on both an individual and corporate level. The House of Prayer is biblical and for today. The label has been checked. This is a family affair. The sky is not falling, and there is time to change. My resource commitments will likely change. Weakness is valuable. Conflict and resistance may follow, as they have in the past. The gravity of my personal and corporate entering into the House of Prayer paradigm is understood. Repentance has been followed as needed.

Getting started

Let's begin with individual application. Most people understand the modern concept of dieting. It will help illustrate the House of Prayer application. Our current eating and exercise patterns have led to our present-day obese condition in America. Most experts agree that pursuing a fad diet or crash diet has little lasting effect. Since permanent change is the goal, an incremental and long-term managed approach to diet and exercise is best. Success is much higher under these conditions.

This advice will work well in the House of Prayer. Start small and build incrementally yet lean into weakness. Be faithful. There is a place for extravagance, too (Mark 14:3). Have a vision of the destination—a lifestyle of Davidic worship. Meditate on and study the scriptures provided in this book. Grow in your amazement of what God is doing in this hour. When you are home, endeavor to have worship music in the background. If you have the Internet, go to *IHOPKC.org* and turn on the prayer room live-streaming. The IHOPKC prayer room runs 24/7. If that is not available, there is a great deal of worship music available through numerous media resources. Saturate your home with worship. Some radio stations provide segments of uninterrupted worship. (Beware of too much radio chatter. It can be distracting.) Adjust the volume to suit your personal tastes. Learn to study and pray with worship in the background. It will help you prepare for time in the local prayer room where you move in and out of prayer, study and worship.

Look for a House of Prayer in your area. Check out the Internet and remember to look at the label. Plan to spend time there. Start with an hour a week, more if you can, less if you must. If there is no House of Prayer in your area, find the closest one and plan a road trip. Remember, all the Jewish men, regardless of where they lived, had to be in Jerusalem at least three times a year to celebrate God's feasts in His House of Prayer. Find out if your church has a prayer meeting. It may not be a House of Prayer as described here, but it is a great start. Learn to participate in public prayer. Give some portion of time to pray for Israel and God's promises for them. If your church doesn't have a prayer meeting, ask the pastor if you may start one. Find a friend(s) who shares your desire for intercession and worship and invite them to join with you. Start with what you have. Remember Paul's admonition. "For if the readiness is present, it is acceptable according to what *a person* has, not according to what he does not have" (2 Cor. 8:12). Paul was addressing giving, but the principle goes beyond money. If all of this is impractical or simply not available, ask your Father who sees in secret to break in and change the circumstances, and keep praying until He does.

Plant your stake and be unwilling to move it. Commitment to lasting change is difficult. It will take sacrifice. In one sense, it is no different than eating better and exercising more. The dynamics of failure arrayed against you are large. The urge to quit or take shortcuts is huge. This is one reason for the size of the diet-exercise business. The lure of the next big silver bullet in diet management or exercise wizardry is intoxicating. We can't manage ourselves and desperately hope to find that silver bullet that will require little or no commitment yet be enormously successful. Honestly, there isn't a silver bullet. (But there are many who would sell you a silver bullet.) The House of Prayer is inconvenient. Sacrifice is required. Weakness will follow. Opposition should be expected. And we can't walk with a House of Prayer heart and practice without sustained and refreshed commitment. This a marathon race, not a 100-yard dash.

There is no optimum House of Prayer lifestyle. David was a one-thing man. He wanted to dwell in the House of Prayer all the days of his life. And he did get into the House of Prayer morning, noon, and night. He was an incredibly busy man with significant responsibilities—as king (president, chief justice, and majority leader), husband, father of many, military man, and lover of God. On the surface, his desire for the House of Prayer and his responsibilities may appear absolutely incompatible, but all things are possible with God. The House of Prayer is the wineskin of God's House, and our giftings and callings and assignments should integrate with the House of Prayer according to the Spirit's direction.

Some of the Levites had the House of Prayer as a full-time occupation. Naturally, they spent the majority of their time there. Everyone else has to wrestle with God's balance. God does not see an incompatibility. The vast majority of saints are like David. They will have to catch time in the House of Prayer as they can. Naturally, seasons of life have a great impact on our availability. This is absolutely okay. It needs to be managed, but God gives us the seasons of life. Maintaining a Davidic heart is at the root of the House of Prayer. Actual time spent will vary. Those who spend little time in prayer today will be lovingly challenged by the Lord.

For a limited number of people, moving into a House of Prayer lifestyle may not look much different than how they spend their lives today. They love Jesus and are already running flat out for Him. They have a ministry from Him. The Holy Spirit will suggest the appropriate level of change, however small that may turn out to be. The House of Prayer heart will continually monitor the time, treasure, and talent expenditures with a view to being in God's House as God directs. They want their family, church, and city to have the full dividend.

The corporate application is different than personal application. The individual has a great deal of control over his own life, but once that person steps into a church or ministry, then promoting organizational change becomes a matter of prayer and humility. Adoption takes time. God changes people. And churches and organizations are collections of people. God is the primary mover, and night and day prayer according to David is a very effective way to agree with God. When we agree with God, He releases His Word. Change follows for individuals, ministries, and churches. The Lord grows what is His. Don't forget waiting and adversity. God's timetable is perfect.

It should be noted that family is a special type of corporate application. Not much is known about children in the House of Prayer. Jehoshaphat brought families—even infants—into the courts to pray when the country was threatened by the kingdom of Ammon and company. Presumably there should be planned opportunity for the children (2 Chron. 20:13). Jesus certainly had a high view of children and their participation. Jesus Himself was in the temple courts—the place of prayer—when He was twelve. The House of Prayer should be family-friendly. Growing up in the House of Prayer and developing a House of Prayer heart at an early age agrees well with Moses' instructions to fathers. Teach them diligently. Young singers and musicians will emerge and joyfully carry the House of Prayer. It is a compelling vision of what the House of Prayer can become.

However, spouses and children may not be on the same page, even as church boards, elders, pastors, and congregations may not be able to grasp the need for a House of Prayer. The individual in this setting will need to let God handle House of Prayer promotion. House of Prayer activities must be carved out with care. God is not interested in ending marriages, families, or churches over House of Prayer commitments. He works very well in secret (Matt. 6:6). Waiting on and for God is an essential House of Prayer attribute. God will test our desire to wait for Him, and some of the first testing comes in the family. Pray. Wait for the Lord. God is never late.

Churches should follow the same approach as individuals. Start small. Teach the scriptures. Gather musicians and intercessors. Find a weekly time on the calendar to start. Even an hour a week is great. Plant your stake. Leaders must be engaged. The church is accustomed to following the leaders. If the leader does not have a conviction surrounding the call for 24/7 prayer and worship, he needs to return to the scriptures to get such a conviction or wait for the Lord to provide one, and the House of Prayer individuals should pray for their leaders.

The biblical model is Davidic worship—the night and day corporate offering that mixes instrumentally supported worship and intercession before the face of the Lord, according to the heavenly pattern given King David (1 Chron. 28:19). It is agreement with God in declaration and song. Worship—declaring God's attributes, and intercession—declaring God's purposes in the earth, flow from the Scriptures, God's testimony. The worshipers remind God what He has written and promised in His Word and they call forth its fulfillment. This partnership with the Master is offered from a forgiven and intimate heart and generates the remarkable and deeply satisfying experience of the Master. This service *to* and joyful experience *of* the Master is called the *sharath* of the Lord, which in turn drives out a missions outreach to the nations—drawing all men with marvelous signs—to come in awe and dwell in His courts.

Beyond this basic, there is latitude on how Davidic worship is done and managed. Denominations and churches have specific worship and intercession patterns. The House of Prayer is not a call for everyone to be the same. The Bible won't change. Interpretation may fluctuate, but application will most likely be different across the body of Christ. This is a good thing.

Cities – God's priority and joy

The citywide church is a critical corporate application. God's specific interest and focus on cities adds a further dimension to the House of Prayer. In the past, a congregational vision for the city meant, "Come to our church." A true citywide vision stretches everyone. Humility and grace must be in great supply. Every church will have a struggle with "They are not like me." Denominational churches may have a further struggle because they don't usually have local autonomy to make decisions. The end of the age and a drive for a shared House of Prayer in a city or region will definitely test John 13:35: "By this all men will know that you are My disciples, if you have love for one another." Few congregations would have the resources to carry a true 24/7 House of Prayer. Sharing this burden and challenge across a city will be the greatest challenge and one of its greatest benefits.

God had certainly chosen David and chosen Jerusalem, but would He choose other locations to hear His words? Does God care about other cities? Absolutely! God used the king of Assyria to discipline nations and cities. Two hundred years later, He used the Babylonians to do the same. Jeremiah saw the destruction of Damascus and gave us understanding into God's heart concerning this city when he quotes God as calling Damascus "the city of my joy!" (Jer. 49:25; KJV). What an amazing description. Damascus routinely got mixed up in attacks against Israel and was full of intrigue. Yet God described it as the city of His joy!

Jesus makes a startling statement concerning several cities in Galilee and surrounding nations. In the days of Abraham, the city of Sodom was completely destroyed because ten righteous men could not be found there (Gen. 18:32). If the miracles that had been performed in Chorazin, Bethsaida, and Capernaum during the ministry of Jesus had been done in Sodom, that city would not have been swept away. The judgment of Tyre and Sidon, two Phoenician cities, would be more tolerable than the judgment passed on the Israelite cities mentioned above. Does God have joy over other cities that eventually and sadly perish because of sin? This must pain God! Would the result be different if there was a citywide House of Prayer as David envisioned—drawing men into His courts with attending signs and wonders?

> Bless the LORD, O my soul, And all that is within me, *bless* His holy name. Bless the LORD, O my soul, And forget none of His benefits; Who pardons all your iniquities, Who heals all your diseases; Who redeems your life from the pit, Who crowns you with lovingkindness and compassion; Who satisfies your years with good things, *So that* your youth is renewed like the eagle. The LORD performs righteous deeds And judgments for all who are oppressed. (Ps. 103:1-6)

If Davidic worshipers were located in the cities of the earth and prayed like David in Psalm 103 for those cities night and day, would the outcome be different? Would they encounter the gracious God who releases marvelous benefits? Would the enemies of the city be confused and distressed as a result of the operation of the House of Prayer as Jehoshaphat discovered? Would dread fall on the unrighteous? The House of Prayer has implications for cities. Remarkably, the Greek word for church used by the New Testament writers is *ekklesia*. In Greek culture, it was the "assembly of the *demos* [the people assembled] in Athens and in most Greek *poleis* [cities]" (TDNT, Vol 3, 513). The church is the collection of saints in a city. And the revelation of John was written to the churches in seven cities. The city is part of the assignment for the church of that city!

All the nations will eventually turn against God's plans (Zech. 12:3; Joel 3:2). Egypt is one of those countries. However, there will be city exceptions. Isaiah mentions five such Egyptian cities that will follow the Lord (Isa. 19:18) in the last of the last days. There are approximately 195 countries in the earth (Infoplease, accessed 2014), while the number of cities in the world varies dramatically, based on the definition used. And both sets of numbers continue to change.

God is looking for a *perhaps*—an opportunity for mercy, in the cities of the earth. Will there be other city exceptions? Perhaps if there are Houses of Prayer in the cities of the earth, the outcome may be changed. Incense altars—the place of 24/7 prayer—will be in multiple locations, according to Malachi 1:11, and will fill the nations. What about your city or the city near you?

In developing a citywide House of Prayer, it might be helpful to take a page from Solomon's playbook. He appointed deputies from each of the twelve tribes (1 Kgs. 4:7). Each month the deputy in charge made sure Solomon's table and household in Jerusalem had everything it needed.

There are 168 hours in the week. *Night and Day Prayer According to David* assumes the presence of musicians throughout the day. Most singers and musicians can comfortably minister for two hours. If this is a reasonable expectation, then the week could be broken down into eighty-four two-hour segments. Houses of prayer that are operating today call this two-hour segment a watch. If there were eighty-four churches in a city or region and they all agreed to support one watch a week, much as the tribes supported Solomon's house, it would be possible for a city or region to have a fully functional House of Prayer. No doubt a church might struggle with an after-midnight watch or perhaps an afternoon watch. The sacrifice and resulting weakness would not go unnoticed. Pastoral care for watch teams would stay with the churches, and the House of Prayer could focus on citywide prayer.

A local church could provide the singers, musicians, intercessors, and intercession theme for the two-hour watch. Everyone in the community would be welcome. The Levites lived on the tithes of the people, and Aaron's descendants lived on the tithe of Levites (Num. 18:24). The citywide House of Prayer could be funded and supported in the same fashion. Local churches would, in effect, tithe their time, treasure, and talent to the citywide House of Prayer for citywide impact. Most ministries in a city are familiar with reaching across congregational lines in some measure, and that style of governance may be most helpful for a citywide House of Prayer.

Larger churches could certainly fully man and support a House of Prayer on their own, but smaller churches might even find a weekly commitment difficult to manage. Moses' instruction on gathering manna is helpful (Ex. 16:17-18). Some gathered more. Some gathered less. But there was no lack. God will orchestrate His House of Prayer.

The church has one other responsibility. Make disciples. A great harvest is coming and may have already started. New believers from the beginning must understand God's call for intimacy and, where possible, be introduced to a local House of Prayer. This practice should fit snuggly in between growing in our understanding of the scriptures, being baptized, connecting with a church, and sharing the good news with others. Henry Ford made the famous statement, "If you always do what you've always done, you'll always get what you've always got" (Ford, 2015, accessed November 2015). It is time for a change.

Participating in a House of Prayer in some dimension should become the new normal for believers and be introduced to young believers or returning prodigals at the earliest opportunity. Likewise, mission agencies should include House of Prayer development in their planning and execution. The great devotion must precede and fuel up the great commission. The business world understands that it is better to do it right the first time than have to redo it later and incur all the additional costs. The church must understand this as well. It takes a little more effort and focus on the front end of discipleship but yields better results over the long haul.

Much has been made in recent years about the desire for unity in the church and among churches. Our cities need prayer to protect against the enemy who wants to come in and against the enemy that has already come through the unguarded gates and is actively fomenting strife. Our cities need the benefits of a House of Prayer to drive out the great commission. Something amazing happens in the House of Prayer when we are committed to pray as commanded by David. We not only fall further in love with Jesus, but we actually begin to love and like the people we pray with— even those who view the world differently. What the church has pursued and found so elusive surfaces nicely in the context of the dedicated pursuit of intimacy and night and day prayer according to David.

One final story may be helpful.

Chapter Twenty-Three

EPILOGUE

I magine living in a bedroom community nestled on a beautiful bluff overlooking the ocean. Life moves in a comfortable routine. Work, play, and family continue as they always have. Homeowners make modest repairs to keep their houses functional and safe. Normal changes occur as the community ebbs and flows with changing times. Neighbors help each other as needed and life is good.

But then a threat shows up on the distant horizon. Stories of alarming weather patterns and storm surges are beginning to show up in the news. Polar ice is beginning to melt. Higher sea levels are resulting in serious erosion around the world. Residents in the community are starting to see evidence of this erosion at the bottom of their own bluff. This had always been a potential issue for the community, but had seemed a farfetched and very unlikely threat. In fact, no one had thought it could ever really happen. Over the 100 years or so that people had lived in this community, stronger safety codes had been recommended but few families had ever implemented them. The codes had been confusing and enforcement had been lax. In general, people had built what and where they wanted in the neighborhood. Now, however, erosion was beginning to look like it could be a true threat to the community.

Some community members believe that this new threat is overstated and become angry at the idea of being required to make changes. They choose to ignore the growing signs of trouble. Others who raise concerns are ridiculed in private and in public as troublemakers. They are sure that his threat is temporary and manageable and will eventually pass. They are eternally optimistic and announce that the community will do fine. There is no need to be concerned or overreact. A unified cry to gather and address the threat is ignored. The city siren is not blaring.

Those, however, who take the concerns seriously go back and do their homework. They investigate erosion rates at other oceanside communities. They discover to their alarm that the erosions around the world are truly increasing at a devastating rate. And it is not slowing down. The new building codes suggested years earlier had indeed been valid. These few community members scramble to update and shore up their foundations. They recognize that their current foundations and locations are unsafe. They see taking action as the only right option, even though it will create hardship for them. Since they love the homes they have, they determine to move their homes to higher ground—literally. The make elaborate and costly arrangements to have their homes lifted and put on special flatbed trucks and moved up the hill to newlly constructed foundations well out of harm's way.

It is not an easy move. The new foundations have to be built to specification and homeowners have to make adjustments to their homes. The heating, air-conditioning, plumbing, electrical, and all the supports have to be adjusted to match the new foundations. Frames have to be trued up to sit squarely on the foundation. This is a costly remedy. Some make all the changes immediately. Some realize starting over is the best approach. Others begrudge the move, procrastinate, complain, and choose to put off all the required hookups and adjustments. They do the minimum, so they can quickly return to their work and play.

Then one day it begins to rain. And it rains for 8 days straight. With horror, the residents watch as the bluff begins to break off and fall into the ocean. Before their very eyes, several houses literally fall over the bluff. Time has run out. The siren is now blaring. Leaving behind their work and play, others quickly make necessary changes. Now everyone helps each other. Lives are clearly at stake. The sky is indeed falling.

It soon becomes a community-wide disaster, bigger than anyone thought it would be. Those who took the signs and warnings seriously are in a position to help others who didn't. They do what they can.

So too, God is going to redo the foundation of His church. A great storm is coming in these last days, and He will call His church back to His original building codes. The Cornerstone, Jesus, will stay in His place, and all that the prophets and apostles taught will remain unchanged. But the rest of the edifice of the church will be lifted up, and a House of Prayer foundation will be inserted under every church that belongs to Him. Times of refreshing will come to a repentant church. The churches will have to make adjustments in their structures and ministries to sit correctly on the House of Prayer foundation. All their programs, time, treasure, and talent allocations will need to be reviewed to line up with the restored tabernacle of David.

There is still time, but it is running out, and churches can and should help one another. The Bible says that the nations will turn against God, but nothing is said about the cities of the earth. Communities can say yes to the Lord. Collectively, congregations own the cities in which they live. He has pre-positioned His saints around the globe and is listening as He promised He would. The flood has not come in force yet, but it will. God announced His plans in advance to allow His children time to prepare.

There will be cities on the earth that will experience an unusual degree of mercy. Trouble will be everywhere, but God will have cities where folks can flee and find salvation, healing, hope, provision, and other kingdom benefits. Houses of Prayer will drive these cities and hold the gates.

This is a good news story. The saints will have a tremendous testimony and will even go out into all the world to search for the lost so the marriage feast will be full. Signs and wonders will occur. There will be many victorious martyrs who will die well in the Lord, and many who will experience God's fatherly love and phenomenal deliverance. They will continue to testify and dwell in God's courts.

There will be cities on a hill. There will be shining lights and a great harvest. The end time bride will be equally yoked and made lovely by the Bridegroom, who will use night and day intimacy, intercession, and worship, and the *sharath* of the Lord to accomplish His purposes. The bride will get ready and hasten the day.

REFERENCES

Adamson, Dr. Ian. *The valley of the angels. http:// www.impalapublications.com/blog/index.php?/ archives/5335-11-The-Valley-of-the-Angels,-by-Cllr-Dr-Ian-Adamson-OBE.html*; Accessed 12/17/2010.

Anderson, Mark 2012. Onething Conference. *MikeBickle.org*.

Barna, George. 2001. *Annual study reveals America is spiritually stagnant*. Barna Research Group. *http://www. barna.org/barna-update/article/5-barna-update/37-annual-study-reveals-america-is-spiritually-stagnant?q=spent+prayer* (accessed December 11, 2010).

_____. 2004. *Religious beliefs remain constant but subgroups are quite different*. Barna Research Group. *http:// www.barna.org/search?q=evangelical* (accessed August 18, 2011).

_____. 2005. *Barna reviews top religious trends of 2005*. Barna Research Group. *http://www.barna.org/barna-update/article/5-barna-update/166-barna-reviews-top-religious-trends-of-2005?q=evangelical+prayer* (accessed December 11, 2010).

Bickle, Mike. 2003. Contending for the Power of God. *MikeBickle.org*

_____ 2013. Onething Conference. *MikeBickle.org*

Bounds, E. M. 2010 *#4 Tendencies to be avoided. http://prayerfoundation.org/booktexts/z_embounds_powerthroughprayer_00_index.htm* (accessed December 11, 2010).

Bradford, John. 1550. *https://en.wiktionary.org/wiki/there_but_for_the_grace_of_God_go_I* (accessed May 28, 2016).

Brown, F., Driver, D., Briggs, C. 1975 *Hebrew and English Lexicon of the Old Testament.* Clarendon Press: Oxford, England.

Bureau of Labor Statistics. 2012. American Time Use Survey–2011. USDL-12-1246, *https://www.bls.gov/news.release/archives/atus_06222012.pdf* (accessed May 28, 2016).

Cahill, Thomas. 1995. *How The Irish Saved Civilization.* New York, NY: Doubleday.

Catholic Communities of Prayer. 2011. *http://catholiccommunitiesofprayer.org/the_unum_necessarium* (accessed January 21, 2011).

Dyck, Drew. 2010. "The leavers: Young doubters exit the church." Chri*stianity Today* Vol. 54, no. 11 (November). *http://www.ctlibrary.com/ct/2010/november/27.40.html* (accessed December 11, 2011).

Farmer, Sharon, and Barbara H. Rosenwein, eds. 2000. *Monks & Nuns, Saints and Outcasts: Religion in Medieval Society.* Ithaca, NY: Cornell University Press.

Ford, Henry. *http://www.goodreads.com/quotes/904186-if-you-always-do-what-you-ve-always-done-you-ll-always* (accessed November 24, 2015).

Friedrich, Gerhard. 1971. *Theological Dictionary of the New Testament*. Vol. 3. Grand Rapids, MI: Eerdmans.

_____ 1971. *Theological Dictionary of the New Testament*. Vol. 4. Grand Rapids, MI: Eerdmans.

_____ 1971. *Theological Dictionary of the New Testament*. Vol. 7. Grand Rapids, MI: Eerdmans.

Infoplease. 2014. *http://www.infoplease.com/ipa/A0932875.html* (Accessed July 13, 2014).

Keil, C. F., and F. Delitzcsh. 1975. *Commentary on the Old Testament*. Vol. 5. Grand Rapids, MI: Eerdmans.

Osborne, Grant. 2008. *Revelation*. In *Baker Exegetical Commentary of the New Testament*. Grand Rapids, MI: Baker Academic

NIV Study Bible. Kenneth L. Barker, gen. ed. 10th anniversary ed. Grand Rapids, MI: Zondervan, 1995. Print.

Pew Forum. 2018. How the religious typology groups compare. *The Pew Forum on Religion and Public Life. https://www.pewforum.org/interactives/how-the-religious-typologies-compare/?issue=prayer* (accessed December 12, 2019).

Preston, John 2004. On our knees. *The Teal Trust. http://www.prayerguide.org.uk/prayersurvey.pdf* (accessed December 11, 2011).

Przybylski, Debbie. 2015. "THE INCREASE OF HOUSES OF PRAYER WORLDWIDE." *http://nations-hop.org/the-increase-of-houses-of-prayer-worldwide* (accessed May 20, 2020).

Ravenhill, Leonard. 1962. *Revival praying*. Minneapolis, MN: Bethany Fellowship Inc.

Richardson, Rick. 2000. Evangelism Outside The Box. Downers Grove, Illinois: InterVarsity Press.

Ulster Archaeological Society. 2010. *Ulster journal of archaeology*, Volume 1. *http://books.google.com/books?id=-bAJKAAAAYAAJ&pg=PA169&lpg=PA169&dq=%22A+place+it+was,+truly+sacred,+the+nursery+of+saints+who+brought+forth+fruit+most+abundantly+%22&source=bl&ots=SqFVPP5w1p&sig=VihJ2CFhrU3ZFV3y0n2ebQLqI7U&hl=en&ei=nLcUTfjMMJHBngeCk_i7Dg&sa=X&oi=book_result&ct=result&resnum=1&ved=0CBMQ6AEwAA#v=onepage&q=%22A%20place%20it%20was%2C%20truly%20sacred%2C%20the%20nursery%20of%20saints%20who%20brought%20forth%20fruit%20most%20abundantly%20%22&f=false* (accessed December 24, 2010).

Waugh, Geoff. 2011. *Power from on high. http://www.openheaven.com/library/history/zinzendorf.htm* (Accessed 4/2/2011).

Wikipedia. *Diffusions of Innovation. http://www.ask.com/wiki/Diffusion_of_innovations?o=2801&qsrc=999&ad=doubleDown&an=apn&ap=ask.com.* (Accessed 10/29/2014.)

CPSIA information can be obtained
at www.ICGtesting.com
Printed in the USA
FSHW020516241020
75053FS